Negotiation: A Very Short Introduction

T0016877

VERY SHORT INTRODUCTIONS are for anyone wanting a stimulating and accessible way into a new subject. They are written by experts, and have been translated into more than 45 different languages.

The series began in 1995, and now covers a wide variety of topics in every discipline. The VSI library currently contains over 700 volumes—a Very Short Introduction to everything from Psychology and Philosophy of Science to American History and Relativity—and continues to grow in every subject area.

Very Short Introductions available now:

Available soon:

For more information visit our website

www.oup.com/vsi/

Carrie Menkel-Meadow

NEGOTIATION

A Very Short Introduction

OXFORD
UNIVERSITY PRESS

Great Clarendon Street, Oxford, OX2 6DP,
United Kingdom

Oxford University Press is a department of the University of Oxford.
It furthers the University's objective of excellence in research, scholarship,
and education by publishing worldwide. Oxford is a registered trade mark of
Oxford University Press in the UK and in certain other countries

First edition published in 2022

Impression: 1

Published in the United States of America by Oxford University Press
198 Madison Avenue, New York, NY 10016, United States of America

British Library Cataloguing in Publication Data
Data available

Library of Congress Control Number: 2022933345

ISBN 978-0-19-885140-0

Printed in the UK by
Ashford Colour Press Ltd, Gosport, Hampshire

*For Robert, practitioner of problem-solving
negotiation for 50 years*

Contents

Preface and acknowledgments

Humans have been negotiating since they came into existence. Studying negotiation is newer. Although people negotiate with themselves, their partners, their families, their communities, with merchants in markets and in groups, it is when larger groups, like nation-states, negotiate with each other that we look to theories of action and strategy—what are our goals and what means should we use for peace-seeking, national gain, and diplomacy.

As a field, negotiation draws on the knowledge bases of many fields: political science, psychology, economics, history, sociology, anthropology, law, and game theory, decision science, policy planning, and leadership studies. It also draws on multi-disciplinary and empirical studies of human behavior, including cognitive, social, and behavioral psychology and economics and gender, race, ethnicity, and class studies. We want to know what to do to be more effective negotiators in the many contexts in which we encounter or need others to accomplish something we cannot do on our own. This is not a "how to" book, but a book about how to think about negotiation and its contextual complexities.

The field of negotiation is marked by different frameworks and theories about whether our goals are to maximize our own gains or seek joint gain and betterment for all. This VSI surveys these different approaches so the reader can assess what makes sense in particular contexts. Our view is that "one size will not fit all" and the well-informed negotiator will choose goals, frameworks, strategies, and behaviors that are appropriate to the situation, all while considering what the other parties to the negotiation are thinking about too. Negotiation has always been an interactive and dynamic human process—but now it may even be more than human—humans plus machines.

It is challenging to distill decades of social science and hundreds of years of human experience into a slim volume, but this book should whet the appetite of any person who wants to learn more. There is an extensive reading list at the end, as well as an Appendix for use in planning future negotiations.

I have been teaching and writing about negotiation for over 40 years and practicing it even longer as a child, sister, wife, aunt, lawyer, teacher, consultant, consumer, and mediator. My first learning about and then teaching negotiation could not have flourished without the colleagueship, mentorship, and friendship of Howard Raiffa, James Sebenius, Michael Wheeler, Roger Fisher, Larry Susskind, Frank Sander, Paul Brest, Deborah Kolb, Alain Verbeke, Robert Mnookin, Howard Gadlin, Orna Rabinovich-Einy, Amy Cohen, Carol Liebman, Stephanie Smith, Janet Martinez, Michael Palmer, Simon Roberts, Margaret Shaw, Russell Korobkin, Melanie Greenberg, Bea Moulton, Gary Bellow, Joel Lee, Susan Gillig, and Mark Spiegel; co-authorships with Andrea Kupfer Schneider, Jean Sternlight, Lela Love, Michael Moffitt, Maria Moscati, Christopher Honeyman, Emmanuel Vivet; and enriching mutual student–teacher relationships, from around the world, with Kondi Kleinman, Peter Reilly, Clark Freshman, Janis Nelson, Lukasz Rozdeiczer, Letizia Coppo, Rutger Metsch, Ana Silva, Carlos Ruffinelli, Carlos Silva, Ana Carolina Viella Riella, and other bright stars in a stellar universe.

This book is far better (and shorter) for the careful and serious review of Naomi Creutzfeldt, Kondi Kleinman, and my best negotiation partner, Robert Meadow. Thanks to my research assistant Alexandra Cadena, faculty assistant Maria Gonzalez, and librarian extraordinaire Dianna Sahhar. With great appreciation for OUP for support and careful editing—Andrea Keegan, Jenny Nugee, Luciana O'Flaherty, and Imogene Haslam.

May you go forth and negotiate good arrangements and solve problems with what you learn in this book.

Carrie Menkel-Meadow
Los Angeles, California

List of illustrations

List of illustrations

List of tables

Chapter 1
When we need others to accomplish something

Consider each of these scenarios: Two young children both want the last piece of chocolate cake. Their mother says she will cut it down the middle and they can share. Is there a better way? You see an antique ring in a flea market that you like. The seller offers a price that is more than you are willing to pay. He says, you drove here on a tank of gas that cost more than this ring. Don't you think a permanent item is worth more than the gasoline you use? What can you do to get a better price? Many countries would like to limit the production of nuclear material for weapons components in Iran and North Korea. How should they conduct negotiations with many parties? These examples, and so many others, are the everyday and major international negotiations we face as we approach others to get what we and they need and want.

Everyone negotiates. Whenever any person, couple, community, company, organization, or country needs someone else to accomplish something, they must negotiate—*seeking agreement with one or more people to do that which one cannot do alone*. We also often negotiate internally with ourselves about whether to do something or not (if I go to the gym this morning, can I have dessert this evening?). So negotiation is also a form of decision making—where we ask ourselves: "what should I do in particular situations?"

Sometimes negotiations are designed to create something new—a relationship, a treaty, a new entity, partnership, contract (called a transactional or *deal negotiation*). Other times negotiations are used to resolve conflicts, resolving past disputes or providing for future relations, including ending relationships—think Brexit or divorce (called *dispute negotiation*). Governmental negotiations create new laws and regulations (*legislative negotiations*). We negotiate in our families, in our workplaces, when we buy something, when we want to begin or end a relationship, and when we want to solve a problem with others. Individuals negotiate, as do their representatives (lawyers, agents, brokers, parents, guardians). Organizations and entities (e.g. corporations, trade unions, non-profit organizations, universities) negotiate (both internally with their members, employees, and externally with their customers, constituencies, competitors, suppliers, and regulators). Countries negotiate with each other to form treaties on substantive engagements, including economic relations, environmental undertakings, arms reduction, cooperation on criminal matters and to prevent conflicts (providing for peaceful means of dispute resolution to prevent aggression) or end them through peace agreements following war. Governments negotiate with their citizens, with other governments, and, of course, internally with themselves in legislative-parliamentary negotiations; political party negotiations; political sub-divisions, including states, provinces, and municipalities; and inter-governmental agency and branch negotiations. In short, humans need to work with other humans to accomplish their goals, to survive, and to flourish—by making things better than they were before negotiation occurs.

Many people think of negotiation as an anxiety-producing process because we don't know where we will wind up at the end. Others find argument, persuasion, and pursuit of a good deal thrilling. But negotiation is more than a complex and sometimes fraught process of human interaction. It is at the same time both a *conceptual* matter of *analyzing* what is at stake, and then later a *behavioral process* of choices for action, comprising offers, proposals, arguments, question asking, suggestions, threats, claims, information, and solutions. Because, by definition, negotiation involves interaction with others, both *analysis* (conceptualizing the issues being negotiated) and *behavior* are dynamic works-in-progress and must be revised before, during, and after engagements and processing of new information. Most successful negotiations result in an agreement, in a *contract*, *treaty*, or *memorandum of understanding*, but some are informal understandings. Many may have "reopener" or "contingency" agreements to permit renegotiation when conditions or facts change. How we hold people, countries, and entities to their agreements by enforcement may involve further negotiations, court action, or referral to some other process of dispute resolution.

Conventional conceptions of negotiation are that they are often competitive processes in which each party tries to maximize its own interests, assuming scarcity of resources (money, land, even identity) which must be divided (called a problem of *distributive bargaining*; a *"zero-sum game"* in which your gain of a dollar or acre is my loss). And a conventional (and lazy) conception of negotiation is that it will end through a compromise or a "splitting the difference" resolution. But, how we *think* of the negotiation problem (conceptualizing or the *"science"* of negotiation) depends on many factors—what is at stake, who are the parties, how many issues there are, what is the context or industry in which the negotiation is situated— and determines how we *act*, or the *"art"* of negotiation.

Not all negotiation problems are the same and no one set of analytic or behavioral choices serves in all situations. When parties work *collaboratively* to achieve joint gain, they are using *integrative bargaining* conceptions and behaviors. Negotiation offers the opportunity to make things better than they were before—making lemonade or lemon pie out of lemons.

1. Diplomatic negotiation—Deng Xiaoping and Margaret Thatcher.

In the last few decades, negotiation has emerged as a formal field of study in many different disciplines. Even schoolchildren now learn how to negotiate more effectively, to "use your words" to prevent, manage, or resolve conflict in more effective, less violent ways.

The constituent fields of negotiation contribute to a variety of new processes for human beings to resolve their differences and solve problems—mediation, consensus building, restorative justice, truth and reconciliation commissions, problem-solving courts, and other hybrid processes that enable groups of people to choose how they want to interact to effectively deal with each other.

Negotiation, as a discipline of study, has developed its own concepts, memes, and frameworks to help students and practitioners of negotiation learn how to create value or "expand the pie" (before it is cut into slices), how to cut the cake (if I like the frosting and you the cake, we can both get 100 percent of what we want), create new options and opportunities for joint gain, and to learn to share with future generations. Often, but not always, we will want to "get the best price" by competing, but most negotiations have more than one issue which means that learning how to *trade* effectively means both you and your counterpart can improve your pre-negotiation situation. This is not necessarily "win–win," but "better than before" negotiation. The magic of a good negotiation is that by taking the needs, wants, and interests of all parties into account we can be additive and creative in getting what we want, as much as possible, while also allowing other parties to do well.

What's in a negotiation

Negotiations begin with a mindset or perspective on what is to be accomplished, which in turn affects the choices we make about how to behave, so we must consider different models and conceptual frameworks (note I did not say "styles") of negotiation. This is the "science" of negotiation. We always ask first: what is at *stake* in the negotiation? *What* is the *res* (thing) about which we are negotiating? Is it a scarce resource, or something that can be shared? Can something new emerge from the negotiation (think the American constitution of 1787)? *How many* issues are there to be negotiated? *Who* are the parties? How many parties are there? *When* do we need an agreement? (Now? Can it wait for new information?) *Where* are we negotiating? (Different legal rules in different jurisdictions? A bucolic retreat or a hostile courtroom?) Most importantly, *Why* are we negotiating? Are we buying or selling, creating a law or new entity, ending a war, beginning or ending a business or personal relationship? Can we *solve a problem by negotiating*? This is the analysis of any negotiation that must occur before we can decide how to act. There are more choices than just *competing* or *cooperating*—there are "mixed" or hybrid models of negotiation and sometimes sequential choices will have to be made.

We will also explore the basic concepts that illuminate some of the more universal aspects of negotiation: how the "framing" of a negotiation and the proposals that are made in the beginning affect the negotiation, how to analyze what the possible "Zone(s) of Possible Agreement" (ZOPAs) are; how to place negotiation analysis in the context of what else is possible (alternatives both inside and outside of the negotiation, known as **B**ATNAs, **W**ATNAs, **A**TNAs and **M**LATNAs—**B**est, **W**orst, **A**ll and **M**ost **L**ikely **A**lternatives **T**o a **N**egotiated **A**greement). We consider how to analyze whether a negotiation has "succeeded," not just by evaluating its outcome, but also its process, that is, how did we get "there" and was there a better way to get "there"?

Negotiations are not all the same. Beware of those books that tell you "Winning at All Costs," "You Can Negotiate Anything!," "Splitting the Difference," "Negotiating with the Russians/Chinese/French/Americans," "How to Negotiate Anything With Anyone Anywhere in the World," etc. Negotiations come in different types, sizes, situations, and industries. *Contexts* matter in negotiations—how does the subject matter, industry, setting, materiel, routineness, history of the parties and their relationships to each other (and to others outside the negotiation) affect what is possible or desirable to achieve? Do we need a precedent or publicity? Do we want to keep negotiations private (trade secrets, personal privacy, nondisclosure agreements)? How many parties are involved? Are the parties trying to create, preserve, change, or leave a relationship? Does the status, gender, race, class, age, or profession of the negotiators matter in what they think and do? Are the parties negotiating in person, by phone, via text, instant message, email, or on Zoom? Is the negotiation synchronous or asynchronous?

After the analysis, we come to the negotiating "table" (physical or virtual). What shall we say or do? What are the differences between competing, compromising, cooperating, or collaborating (the 4 Cs of behavioral negotiation)? So we look at the classic

6

dilemmas of negotiation strategy (overall game plan) and tactics (particular behavioral moves). How should we set goals and objectives, who should make the first offers or proposals, should we use an agenda, what research do we need to do, how do we assess what others tell us (how to trust and verify), how do we develop creative solutions to seemingly intractable problems, when do we concede anything, and how do we deal with the competitive "tricks" or bullying tactics our counterparts may use? All of these behavioral choices should be made for a purpose, consistent with planning and goals for the particular negotiation. Behavioral choices cannot be made uniformly or in a vacuum—they are necessarily tied to the contexts and analysis that have preceded any actual engagement with the "other" side(s). Of course, once a negotiator acts and does something, the other side will respond and we will have to consider our next actions. Consider a chess game with potentially infinite moves and countermoves, with the need to react and rethink, but with a clear goal in mind. We consider productive responses, countermoves, and interventions, which include not only the "science" of negotiation but also its "art."

Analysis (Framework)----→Contexts------→Behavior = Process-----→Outcome
Then: Assessment---Evaluation

Even with the best intentions and behaviors, many negotiations fail. Why? Modern research from the disciplines of social and cognitive psychology and behavioral economics helps us to understand why parties often fail to reach agreement when they should have found some accommodation. Most of us make many errors of judgment in receiving and processing information (thinking too "fast or slow" as Daniel Kahneman has documented), in communicating with others, in understanding ourselves and others (what is "rational"; how do emotions both help and impede productive negotiations?), and in reacting without thinking. How can we "correct" for these common human heuristic errors? One answer is to get some help—use a third-party mediator or negotiation expert, agent, broker, or lawyer to facilitate negotiation and "neutralize" the "noise." Modern negotiation theory and practice has correctives for many human processing errors. We can develop ground rules for interactions, set agendas, jointly seek information and data, create task groups, and then determine clear voting and decision rules.

Although most people think of negotiation as two parties butting heads or shaking hands, the modern reality is that most negotiations involve more than two parties, such as the insurance company or governmental agency behind personal injury claims, the lawyers behind any two-party contract dispute, any regional trade agreement, or all environmental treaties, the employees of companies in merger and acquisition negotiations, the family members in any divorce proceedings. With two parties we know we have an agreement when the two parties say yes, but what if there are three parties? Is there an agreement when two say yes and cut out the third? The complexity of negotiations when there are more than two parties adds other issues to consider such as coalition formation, veto powers, holdouts, when we need all to form an agreement. What different approaches, strategies, voting, and decision rules might be required in treaty formation, community and government negotiations, or settlements of aggregate litigation claims. Who goes first? Do I seek out allies from my friends or go to my "frenemies" first? How do we combine different kinds of processes in complex negotiations— principled rationality, rule of law, practical bargains, trades and compromises, emotional, ethical, ideological, and religious commitments and passions when all may be present in a negotiation simultaneously? We need brains (reasons), stomachs (trades of what we "can live with"), and hearts (morals, emotions, and values) to negotiate, all at the same time.

If we reach agreement in any negotiation, how can we be sure the parties will fulfill their commitments? Too often a handshake ends the conversation but is only the beginning of new problems to be resolved. Enforcement of contracts and treaties implicates legal standards and rules which may differ from problem to problem and jurisdiction to jurisdiction. We must understand the legal issues in enforcing agreements in different contexts and understand how to ensure that successful negotiations stay that way, with good monitoring and renegotiation or dispute resolution provisions.

As we consider whether to trust what we are being told, all negotiators must consider their own and counterparts' ethical duties and obligations. Whom do we trust? Formal law provides some answers in contract, tort, and fraud/misrepresentation rules, but there are human, moral, and larger ethical questions that have no easy answer and draw on each negotiator's moral compass. Moral philosophers now debate when we should not "bargain with a devil," as negotiation theorists and practitioners offer advice about how to test for trust and truth telling. As negotiators are we accountable for our work? For the impacts of any negotiation agreement on those not at the table (children in divorce, future generations in environmental or peace negotiations)? When are the goals of negotiation simply "peace" and end of conflict and when should we aim for the more elusive "justice"? When is negotiation (and yes, even compromise) morally or politically compelled for human coexistence and not a sign of weakness?

This short introduction to a vast field ends with consideration of the uses to which the human process of negotiation can (or should) be put. Employing examples from modern international relations, environmental, business, and economic issues we can consider how good negotiation practices might help us address climate change, world peace, health, safety, migration, and other issues facing humanity. This book suggests that the frameworks we choose (distributive division or integrative creative problem solving) for negotiation affect the behaviors we enact, which in turn produce the outcomes we get.

Chapter 2

Frameworks of negotiation: Winning for self or problem solving for all?

It is common for modern negotiation theory and practice to posit two distinct conceptual frameworks for analyzing negotiation—often described as (a) *distributional-adversarial-competitive* negotiation or (b) *integrative-collaborative-problem-solving* negotiation. These two frames assume that one can approach a negotiation in advance, regardless of what the negotiation is about or who the parties are. In fact, there are more than two different frameworks, based on analysis of what the *res/stakes* being negotiated are, *who* the parties are, and a variety of other *contextual factors* that should help us to orient ourselves to choosing both *substantive goals* and appropriate *behaviors* in a negotiation.

The "science" of negotiation suggests that, before we choose the behaviors we will deploy, we must first use *cognitive analysis* of a situation, asking such questions as (1) Is the *res* divisible, sharable, scarce? (2) Do the parties know each other and are they "repeat players" or "one shotters"? (3) How many parties are there? (4) How many issues are involved?

Here we explore four different orientations to negotiation, dependent on answers to these questions. Only then can we consider appropriate *behaviors, the "art" of negotiation* (including separately the *strategies* (plans) and *tactics* (individual behavioral "moves") that fit the negotiation context), as we also consider what our counterparts might be thinking and doing as well.

These frameworks can be succinctly described and illustrated (see Table 1) as (1) *distributive-adversarial-competitive* when the resources being negotiated are limited and must be divided (e.g. money, land); (2) *integrative-problem-solving* where the sharing or expanding of resources or creation of new arrangements or solutions may allow for joint gain for all parties, usually with shared information; (3) *compromising or cooperative-relationship preserving* (when the relationship of the parties may be more important than the substantive outcome, e.g. family, workplace, some business relations, the polity, and even some diplomatic alliances); (4) *mixed* situations where a negotiation setting may allow some problem solving and resource expansion, which then must be allocated (so that the "enlarged" pie will still have to be divided, following some "creating" of resources or new solutions).

Framework # 1 Conventional conceptions of negotiation: The distributional or adversarial model of negotiation

Much negotiation theory and practice can be located in the larger historical zeitgeist in which they have been developed. The concepts behind competitive or distributive negotiation were derived from game theory developed to aid decision making during World War II and the Cold War for strategies for responding to acts of aggression, often without the tools of direct communication. This work had important effects on legal negotiations, advertising, marketing, sales, and the use of win–lose metaphors in social life generally. Thus, "frames" or "memes" are particularly important for understanding when and how different behaviors might be invoked in different settings. For those who have seen negotiation as a competitive activity, metaphors of sports, wars, games, and struggles are legion in

Table 1. Frameworks of negotiation

| | | Frameworks of negotiation | | |
Goal	Model	Behavior	Outcomes
I	Win (Maximizing individual gain)	*Adversarial Distributive/ Competitive*	• Competitive or Positional debate • Arguments/persuasion • Hiding information • Demands • Threats • Deceit • Few concessions	• Win/lose • Impasse • Split the difference
II	Problem solve (Maximizing joint gain)	*Integrative Problem Solving Principled Interest and needs-based*	• Collaborative • Ask questions • Propose suggestions/offers • Listen • Explore needs/interests • Create new solutions/ideas • Brainstorm • Find trades of complementary interests and needs • Use objective criteria, reasons, principles • Have curiosity	• Creative solutions • Expanded issues and opportunities • Contingent agreements

III	Compromise-cooperation (Relationship preserving)	Accommodative Sharing	• Cooperate • Give in • Make concessions	• Compromise • Split the difference
IV	Allocate created resources/solutions	Mixed	• Create, then claim • Trades • Revisit	• Pareto optimal sharing gain • Contingent agreements • Solved problems

descriptions of the process of negotiation and exhortations about how to behave.

For many people, especially those in business or law, the default approach to negotiation is to think of it as a *competition*, in which the goal is to maximize individual gain (higher price for sellers, lower prices for buyers). This mindset to maximize gain or to "win" at negotiation leads to a series of assumptions, which leads to the use of particular behaviors, which in turn often leads to a limited set of outcomes. These assumptions may be appropriate only for some negotiations—such as the simple model of the two-party, one-issue negotiation over price. This simple model is often deceptive as even simple pricing negotiations often have other issues (and other parties) involved which can complicate the possible goals and behavioral choices.

Common assumptions built into an individual maximization goal include the behaviors that one should hide one's real preferences (as revealing them will lead to exploitation by the other side) so that deceit, exaggeration, or misrepresentation are common. Negotiators using this mindset think they can affect outcomes favorably by making high first offers and then using aggressive powers of persuasion and planned limited concessions to keep the outcome close to their desired goal.

We can use such a simple example to define and chart some classic negotiation concepts (Figure 2).

The structure of this picture of distributional or adversarial negotiation is linear. S is one party (assume a seller) and B is the other party (assume a buyer). S has a target price (or an aspiration level—the high price s/he would like to achieve (T(S)) and a resistance point (or reservation price (R(S)) or "bottom line," the lowest price s/he would settle for and still sell the item. On the other side is B (the buyer) who similarly has a target price (a lower value, T(B)) and a reservation price (a higher number but still one

Zone of Possible Agreement (ZOPA)

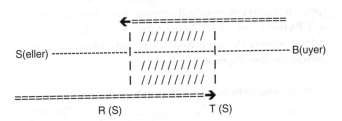

T = Target point (or aspiration point)
R = Resistance point (or reservation price)
/// = Zone of Possible Agreement

2. Zone of Agreement.

B would pay to purchase the item, R(B)). The parties will conclude a negotiation and make a deal within their ZOPA where there is overlap between the values assigned for acceptable ranges of prices. Note that in the chart there is considerable room for an agreement between the Target and Resistance points of the parties. How they allocate what price they will agree to is called the "allocation of surplus value." Here there is ample room for possible agreed-to prices. The competitive-adversarial model suggests that parties make offers of numbers without revealing where they would ultimately settle and the more successful negotiator will be the one who achieves a price closer to its Target price and further away from its Resistance point.

Consider this illustration: Alice the Author has a manuscript to sell—she would like an advance of $10,000 and royalties of 15 percent on all sales (the price). She is negotiating with Columbia Publications and they offer only $5,000 for an advance and 10 percent for royalties. The parties (or their agents/lawyers) may make arguments to each other to justify their offers (the "going rate" for the publisher; the effort put in or the projected sales as arguments made by the author) and eventually they will reach an agreement or not. If this is seen as a single-issue negotiation (price) it is most common for the parties to reach an agreement in a ZOPA that is close to a "split the difference" result, meaning halfway between the first two offers—$7,500 advance and 12.5 percent royalties, expressed as:

$$\frac{O\ (1)\ (\text{offer by Party 1}) + O\ (2)\ (\text{offer by party 2})}{2} = \text{Outcome (midpoint between offers)}$$

Conventional models of distributional negotiations thus suggest that the Author should make a higher demand (raise her aspiration level) so that the ultimate agreement in the middle will be closer to what she hopes to achieve. But the risk of aiming too high (and out of the "authority" of what the publisher can do) is that the publisher may simply walk away (or there will be an impasse in this negotiation).

Ideally a good negotiator here would do her research, know the customary price, and prepare good arguments to suggest why she is better, has worked harder, or deserves more. And she would also benefit from seeking other publishers (what we would call developing *Alternatives to this Negotiated Agreement* or *ATNAs*) to help her decide whether to keep negotiating here or seek a different publication partner. Roger Fisher, William Ury, and Bruce Patton in their paradigm shifting book, *Getting to YES: Negotiating Agreement Without Giving In* (1983) coined the important phrase and concept of having a Best Alternative to a Negotiated Agreement (BATNA) to know when to leave a particular negotiation or to create better alternatives to the negotiation in which one is engaged. We now want to know all the ATNAs (*all the possible alternatives* to this particular negotiation), the WATNAs (the *worst alternatives* to this negotiation—which might cause us to stay in this particular negotiation for want of a better deal) or, most helpfully, the Most Likely Alternative to this Negotiated Agreement (MLATNA)—is there, in fact, a going rate commonly offered by all publishers? What is it most realistic to accept?

But note, even this "simple" single issue, two-party distributive negotiation, is not so simple. The price has at least two components—an advance and a royalty (contingent on sales over time). These two prices could be traded (more advance, lower royalty rate or lower advance, higher royalty rate) depending on the parties' assessments of what they may not fully know now—the contingency of sales as well as their risk tolerance. They could agree to set a price at the beginning (advance) and then assess royalties or adjust them later as they measure sales (contingent agreement). Almost any purchase (e.g. furniture) that might have a discount for all cash now or offer the buyer a zero percent interest rate on a loan for higher total price but lower monthly payment actually has several components. If the Author turns out to be as successful as J. K. Rowling (*Harry Potter*), the publisher will certainly want to keep the contractual relationship going and so may be willing to take a smaller percentage of a larger numerator—the sales. The issue of what kind of relationship the parties are going to have is always on the agenda. If Alice the Author is the next J. K. Rowling there will be other issues to consider: film and product rights—to be negotiated now or later. And there will also be delivery issues in timing, costs, and modes of transfer—both for manuscripts and for furniture.

Thus, conventional advice about aiming high, not revealing true preferences, making demands or strong claims, and making few and small concessions in pricing negotiations (distributive allocations of presumed scarce resources) may be effective in the few cases where there really are scarce resources or one-shot engagements, but most negotiation situations actually involve more issues and more parties. It is often a mistake to look at even a "price" negotiation as being just about "price" unless the objective is clearly a commodity available anywhere from multiple vendors. Consider how one might conceptualize price—a focus on a single price of a unit of a commodity could change if by buying more (quantity, as a second issue), the unit price might be reduced if greater numbers of the item are purchased. And consider how quality may be an issue in any pricing negotiation. Won't Alice the Author care about the quality of the editing of her manuscript (or control over the edits), as the Publisher may want to ensure some performance measures too (quality, timing of production, etc.)?

To decide what is the appropriate approach to have in a negotiation one must always ask these questions first:

Negotiation

1. What is at *stake* (what is the thing involved, scarce resource like money or sharable items)?
2. How many *issues* are there in the negotiation?
3. *Who are the parties, how many* of them (n = 2, n > 2) and are the parties individuals or groups or entities?
4. What do the parties *value* (money, relationship, love, peace, long-term gain)?
5. Are the parties going to have a *relationship* beyond this negotiation (one-off sales, potential longer-term relationship, e.g. supply chain contract, employment, parenting, lawsuit settlement requiring monitoring of performance, diplomatic alliances)?
6. Are the parties *negotiating directly* or using *agents*, brokers, representatives, lawyers, diplomats with their own interests in the negotiation (reputation, payment, incentives, potential conflicts of interest)?

An example of how commitment to the "hardball" school of negotiation can backfire comes from the Covid epidemic. The United States government began negotiating with pharmaceutical giant Pfizer and other drug companies to manufacture vaccines in spring 2020, as the pandemic was reaching extreme numbers in the United States. Although one deal was reached for the US government to purchase 100 million doses (enough to vaccinate 50 million), the US government refused Pfizer's offer to sell more when early trials of the vaccine showed promising results. Pfizer was the only drug company not accepting government subsidies so that it would be free of some government regulations. Pfizer asked the government to invoke the Defense Production Act which would have facilitated a quicker turnaround of manufacturing processes and supply chains. The US government refused and began seeking vaccines from other drug companies. (Nothing wrong with this—the US government was improving its BATNA by seeking other deals.) However, in what can happen in any negotiation, new facts created a more dynamic situation. The Pfizer vaccine was the first to demonstrate effectiveness and so Pfizer was able to sell many doses to European countries, while the US government sought deals with other companies at cheaper prices. Then, when the government later sought to buy more Pfizer doses Pfizer had already committed its available supplies to other countries. As one negotiation commentator noted,

> A competitive mindset and lack of foresight appeared to lead government negotiators to play hardball with Pfizer rather than heeding its early warnings of supply shortages and collaborating on solutions. The focus on recouping investments appeared to distract the White House decision makers from doing all that was needed to enable Pfizer to move full speed ahead with vaccine production…"win–lose" negotiation can distract officials from their responsibility to save as many people as possible.

Consider these variations on single pricing distributive negotiations. A well-known American baseball player Reggie Jackson was negotiating to move teams. He had a top record but he was aging and his future performance was unclear. His agent made a high demand; the desired team responded with a low offer. Confident that this star player would attract many fans to his new team, the agent offered a fixed salary at an acceptable level to the new team plus a "percentage of the gate"—a percentage of ticket sales above last year's attendance (assuming higher attendance attributable to Reggie Jackson). The deal was done and it was successful for all round. Jackson did attract many additional fans. The profit to the team increased as increased sales benefited both parties, turning a simple one-issue salary negotiation into a "contingent" agreement based on different assessments of value and risk. These kinds of adaptation to simple pricing negotiations are now common in many other negotiations (such as actors, directors, and their lawyers getting a percentage of sales from movies, sports, commodities (commissions), commercial leasing (percentage of sales from retail in shopping centers), as well as negotiated rates of commissions on work products, e.g. real estate fees, books, and, in the US, lawyers' contingent fees in lawsuits).

Other examples of assumed scarce resource negotiations that are often considered distributional but don't have to be include land or space. In the Camp David peace talks that resulted in Egyptian and Israeli agreements of mutual diplomatic recognition, a contested issue was the Sinai desert, captured by Israel from Egypt in the Six Day war of 1967. For Egypt the issue was sovereignty (and face-saving, getting its own land back after a loss in war); for Israel the concern was security and safety—preventing future incursions. The classic "split the difference" compromise (sometimes used in border disputes) would not be very effective for a desert land mass with no clear geographic line of division. Instead the land was "demilitarized" with Egyptian "ownership" but no military presence allowed and security surveillance financed in large part by a third party (the United States). The addition of more parties (whether in a mediational stance or as participants in a two-party negotiation) can add solutions, resources, and process interventions that can transform negotiations with assumed limited solutions.

In a different form of scarcity two film stars (Bette Midler and Shelley Long and their agents) competitively argued for "top billing" for a movie (*Outrageous Fortune*, 1987). The top of the marquee seems to be a scarce resource and the negotiations had broken down on this issue. Imagine my surprise when I saw a billboard in Los Angeles with Bette Midler at the "top" and then when I flew to New York I saw Shelley Long's name at the top on a billboard in Times Square. Some clever negotiator had divided the country—Bette Midler (originally from Hawaii) was featured at the top on advertising west of the Mississippi River and Shelley Long (then famous for her role in a TV show, *Cheers*, located in Boston) was at the top of the marquee east of the Mississippi. Now look at all movie credits, opera and ballet programs and see how space may be redesigned (left to right, right to left, top to bottom, bottom to top and with more varied keywords, like "starring", "with," or "featuring") to develop more creative answers to the "who gets top billing?" question.

Distributional arguments about numbers, space, physical, and non-physical items are not always best analyzed as problems of division or competing claims. In the talks between the Soviets and the US for nuclear disarmament (1962–3) negotiations broke down over contested numbers of "inspections" of nuclear production locations without clarification of what an "inspection" actually consisted of or who would do the inspections (as this problem is now revisited with newer nuclear negotiations with North Korea and Iran).

The dangers of the conventional distributional adversarial mindset applied to all negotiations are that most negotiations are not only about numbers but have other issues, whether manifest or latent, so that there are often future consequences to present deals (a deal too harsh may be resisted or revenge sought in other interactions, as many have suggested was true of the Treaty of Versailles's conclusion of World War I). Most significantly, conventional mindsets limit the possible range of negotiated outcomes. In negotiations of legal matters, for example, the parties might think themselves bound by the endowments of the

21

law (or what a court would order if a case goes to trial), which leads to what I have called "the limited remedial imagination of the legal system" (which can adjudicate the past according to legal rules, but can only rarely provide remedies for future engagement), as opposed to negotiating an agreement that can provide more solutions (past and future) for the parties as they design what is best for them (as long as it does not otherwise violate the law).

When parties engage in transactional negotiation (sales, deals, or organizational or entity creation or merger) they may be limited in thinking of conventional "deal points" or boilerplate clauses in contracts that may not fit the particular deal. In one example, a major American movie star asked to have a large Cadillac Escalade provided for his use during filming in Europe because that was "standard" in the contract for his competitive reference group of other movie stars. He successfully negotiated the term. But the filming was in a small European village where the car was too big for the roads and could not be driven. Conventions are appropriate when they fit the situation but negotiations should always be tailored to what is sought to be achieved in a particular matter. General theories must be interpreted through the lens of context to achieve more optimal solutions. Indeed, rather than "narrowing issues" in the hopes of finding agreements, it is often better to expand and have more issues so that issues can be traded to create more possible terms and agreements.

Framework # 2 Integrative negotiation—solving problems for all parties (but not necessarily "win–win")

In an interesting convergence of post-Cold War hopes for peace or more economically productive relations, negotiation was reconceptualized as a problem of coordinating joint gain for both or all the parties to a negotiation. The metaphors and underlying disciplines were expanded. Drawing on work of a multi-disciplinary thinker of the early 20th century, Mary Parker Follett (trained in social work, history, administrative science, labor relations, early organizational development, and business), negotiation theorists and practitioners developed broader orientations to a negotiated problem. For Mary Parker Follett there were three orienting frames for conflicts—domination, compromise, and integration. In a series of examples, she demonstrated that some, if not all, conflict or "friction" could be marshaled to solve problems more creatively. In one example, she was studying in a library and experiencing a draft. She wanted the nearby window closed. But her neighbor felt the air in the library was not circulating sufficiently and wanted the window open. Follett moved to the room next door and opened that window—so air could circulate without a direct draft on her. (Yes, that could raise problems for people in the next room—a new problem of "externalities" created by the solving of one problem by potentially creating problems elsewhere.)

In another set of negotiation problems involving what seem to be divisible items, Follett's underlying principles of seeking to learn parties' real preferences demonstrate how even "scarce" resources can be more effectively (and efficiently) shared. Two sisters are arguing over a single orange. My younger brother and I are arguing over the last piece of the chocolate cake. Mothers, as mediators or arbitrators, tell us to cut the orange or cake in half and share nicely (or she suggests the fairness principle—one cuts, the other chooses). But, as the sisters reveal and I figured out by talking to my brother, when we ask parties what they really want we learn that sometimes the parties value different things, so solutions other than "split the orange/chocolate cake" are possible. The clever mother asks what each party wants, and we learn one sister wants the orange juice, the other wants the zest for a recipe. I like the frosting; my brother likes the cake. When it comes to carrot cake our preferences were reversed—I like the cake, my brother the frosting, so context matters. This is the closest we get in real life to "win–win" (most real-life problems are not win–win), where by cutting the item in a different way both parties get 100 percent, not 50 percent, of what they really want. The lesson here and the basic tool of integrative, problem-solving negotiation is ASK—find out what real preferences are before assuming scarcity or similar interests. Mary Parker Follett used another metaphor to explain her analysis—the "friction" of the bow and violin produces music—conflict can be productive if we know how to use it.

In the 1980s, a new generation of negotiation theorists began to ask different questions of negotiation—not how can we defeat, take advantage of, or "win" "against" the other side, but instead, what is the thing the parties want to do (buy–sell, make a peace treaty, settle a lawsuit, negotiate child custody, preserve the planet) and can we find ways for both/all parties to achieve some gain, or as I prefer to say—*do better as a result of a negotiation than what was available before negotiation.* Not necessarily "win–win," but making lemonade out of lemons (if there is bitter conflict) or making a lemon pie if we are negotiating to make a new thing (transactional negotiation). Thus, we look at a different framework—the possibility of "integrating" the parties' needs and interests to achieve joint gain.

The integrative model of negotiation requires analysis of what is at stake (or could be at stake in the future) in any negotiation and then requires conceptualization of possible solutions or outcomes. Rather than assuming there is something (money or land) to be distributed, we consider what possible other solutions there might be.

Consider the following problem (developed by Stanford engineer James Adams):

Below are three rows of three dots:

Try to connect all the dots with four straight lines, without lifting your pen off the page.

If you are having difficulty, it is because you "see" a box (or a frame, a limited space, or a professional paradigm) that is not really there. The solution is literally, *think outside of the box:*

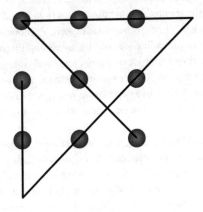

The lines must be drawn "outside" of the box. Now try connecting the dots with only three straight lines:

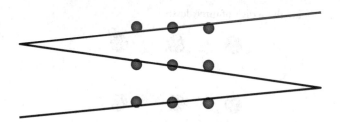

The solution to this exercise is to think "out of the box" which is, in fact, a linguistic or visual "assumption" of a box, or limited space. Once one "sees" outside of the box, the four lines can be drawn from any starting point outside of the box and the lines can be drawn from several different directions. The three-line problem also assumes linguistic and spatial immutable definitions—the lines "connect" the dots by going through them and not assuming the dots must be connected through their "middle."

These types of puzzles are designed for us to realize we can step out of our ordinary professional disciplines (and literal and imagined "spaces") to see other ways to solve a problem. One takes the instructions (draw lines) or parties' needs and interests seriously and then tries to "bring them together" (integrate them), rather than to separate them or divide them in order to solve a problem. Thus, integrative negotiation requires thinking and planning before any kind of encounter with "the other side."

We begin with always asking in each negotiation: What are the parties' real needs, interests, objectives, goals in their negotiation? What are they trying to accomplish? What is the thing about which they are negotiating? Who else might be involved in the dispute, transaction, underlying issue? How many issues are there between the parties? How might these issues be addressed? (Aggregative-all together or separately disaggregated?) When do the parties need to conclude a negotiation—is time of the essence or can time be used to craft contingent or temporary solutions?

Where is the negotiation situated? (This is a particularly important issue for both process (retreat settings, in person, online, public or private) and substance (in legal disputes, the jurisdiction of negotiation might matter for different possible legal outcomes).)

What other possibilities for negotiated outcomes might there be? (Look to other fields of expertise, outsiders to the problem, other sources of creative solutions.)

In short, consider the journalists' six basic questions: Who, What, Where, When, Why, and How as all the factors that may have an effect on the negotiation. The more factors and issues available the more "trades" of preferences will permit more possible solutions to the negotiation.

Consider this illustration: In an anti-trust (anti-competition) lawsuit (class action in the United States) a collection of pharmacies sued drug manufacturers for price fixing. A settlement of over $100 million was reached, which was then objected to by a sub-group of drug retailers which appealed the court-approved settlement. Reallocation of the settlement funds would have been time consuming and costly for all parties. A "solution" was devised in which the drug manufacturers placed a large portion of the settlement into a bank escrow account on behalf of the plaintiffs, which then accumulated interest while the appeal was pending and allowed the drug companies to take a legal corporate tax deduction in that year. By the time the appeal was about to be decided there was enough interest accumulation to pay additional funds to the intervening claimants and the appeal could be dismissed with a full settlement. Here the use of a third party (the bank) and time (accrual of interest as appeal was pending) allowed the available resources to be increased and to allow for a settlement of the matter—a more "creative" negotiation than that which a brittle "win–lose" court result would have accomplished. Many courts in the United States, United Kingdom, Germany,

China, and other countries now require litigants to attempt negotiation or mediation before going to trial—an attempt at more creative and less binary solutions to legal disputes before a court is required to settle differences according to law.

Various ways of thinking more creatively about problem solving and negotiation have been introduced by game theorists, psychologists, decision scientists, and now negotiation scholars and practitioners and others who encourage problem-solving negotiators to consider the following thinking processes to be used in planning for negotiation solutions: uses of analogies and metaphors (direct or fanciful); aggregation/disaggregation or recombinations of elements of a problem; transfer of concepts from other fields or professions; extensions (extending a line of reasoning, principles, or solutions—like those lines outside of the box); challenging assumptions—re-examining what might be "do-able", unpacking clichéd, conventional solutions or ideas; avoiding boilerplate solutions which don't meet the parties' needs; narratives—extending stories, full descriptions of facts or issues; backward/forward thinking—history of the problem, desired future end states, different ways to get "there"; design—planning for future with many alternatives; brainstorming—randomized idea generation without judgment; visualization—use of different competencies and modes of thinking; and reframing—reconsidering different "entry points" to a problem of negotiation.

Problem-solving negotiators seek to avoid the dangers of applying ready-made solutions in transactions as stock terms to negotiated problems. Routine processes and outcomes can be achieved quickly if everyone is playing the same "game," but they may produce "wasteful" solutions (that fail to create more gain by exploring more options). Obviously, the collaboration required to get good information on priorities and facts for creative solution devising may be more time consuming but the payoff may be greater in the robustness of solutions achieved. Note that in this framework of negotiation we use the process word of "collaboration," working together so both (or all in multi-party settings) parties can seek joint gain. This is not a "compromise" or "cooperative" process in which negotiators may concede or "give something up" to the other side to achieve agreement—here we seek to keep constant the needs and interests and priorities of all parties and seek to maximize joint gains.

Framework # 3 Compromise, cooperation, or when the relationship matters more

While many conventional negotiations assume attempts to "win" or take advantage of the other side to accomplish one's own ends, there are many situations in which it is desirable to seek to cooperate with the other parties, indeed to even "give something up" because the goal or values are different—for example, preserving or creating a relationship, whether between people, organizations, communities, and countries. Research has demonstrated that people who know each other (friends, couples, classmates, family members, repeat players at the workplace) often do not "maximize gain" at the expense of their negotiation partners when it is "rational" to place the relationship ahead of any particular argument.

Although compromise has had a reputation in moral philosophy as connoting the giving up of more principled values, in fact, compromise has its own moral value when it is used to further other important values (e.g. the governance of a polity, the preservation of a relationship, to "give" something to one with greater need (sacrifice as a "higher value" in some settings) and also as a decision rule when there is no clear equitable principle for allocation of resources or some form of sharing). Compromise may be appropriate as an efficient ending point for a contested distributional negotiation with parties haggling over a possible impasse or span of values in a bilateral concession pattern (occurring in automobile, house, or other "one-shot" sales) where some agreement is better than none. And, in the examples given above, if the sisters both really do want the orange or my brother and I do both value the whole chocolate cake, a split the difference solution of "sharing" may be a good way to teach children (and adults) that yes, sometimes we do have to share scarce resources. A variation on this sharing theme occurs when people alternate access to a resource or obligations (as in damming of waterways, joint child custody, condominium or co-op (time-share) landownership, or my agreement with my husband, alternating nights—one cooks, the other cleans).

In the political and international sphere, compromise is essential for drafting legislation and making treaties. The technique of "log rolling" allows parties to trade items of different values and put them in a single document to forge an agreement where it might otherwise not be possible (e.g. government budget approvals for different projects). Parties may seek to accommodate each other for a greater cause or relationship, especially if engaging in a contingent agreement that may be modified later, after new data or party re-evaluation. The ability to accommodate or compromise may have its own moral integrity as it is a recognition that the other parties to the negotiation have their own intrinsic human value and need to be acknowledged, a common feature in peace agreements and new forms of transitional justice.

Yet, it is also true that compromises may be wrong or unjustified (most notoriously Chamberlain's compromise at Munich with Hitler) or causing more harm than good. Consider King Solomon's offer to "divide the baby in half" when two mothers claimed the same child. In the biblical story the true mother prevents her real child's death by renouncing her claim to preserve the baby's life. Fortunately, King Solomon's famous "decree" is actually a test to see who values life over contest. In our highly partisan political orders some compromise is clearly necessary for any political actions to be taken (tax, revenue, trade, social welfare, and other policies). Without some "principled" giving in for the greater cause of survival and preservation of the polity, stalemate results and society is not likely to flourish.

Note that the contested frameworks for negotiation replicate one of humankind's oldest philosophical debates—are we essentially selfish and profit maximizing, or do we cooperate for the greater good of the species (or some smaller unit, like the family or our country)? When is it wrong to be too "soft" or too "hard" in our negotiation choices? When should we compete and when should we cooperate and/or collaborate with others? Are we hard-wired to be one or the other, or, as psychologists and sociologists suggest, does the context matter?

Framework # 4 Mixed models: Creating and claiming value; trades, Pareto optimality, and contingent agreements

Many negotiation problems do not reveal themselves analytically at the beginning as distributional or integrative. They are dilemmas, conundrums, or paradoxes. It is often likely that the "moves" of one party will frame the issues between the parties as one or the other, forcing other parties to choose how to react, whether by responding in kind or trying to reframe the situation.

Negotiators can analyze what is at stake to decide what to do in some situations, but often the situations may themselves be more malleable by the negotiators' own frames. And yet, even if there are resources to be shared or expanded, some division may ultimately be required, even of an expanded resource. This is the "mixed" model of negotiation which encourages the integrative, creative processes described above first and then consideration of what division or allocation there might have to be.

Consider the Prisoner's Dilemma from game theory. Two criminal offenders have been arrested and placed in separate cells and offered the following classic negotiation deal (based on Cold War assumptions that there is no form of communication between the parties during the negotiation): "if you confess and incriminate your partner (we need the evidence) you will get a lighter sentence and he a longer one; if you remain silent and your partner confesses, he will get the lighter sentence and you will get a longer one; if neither of you confesses you may get off completely (if we have no other evidence), but if you both confess you will both get full sentences; what do you choose?" As game theorists have demonstrated in countless studies, it is "rational" to defect (or compete) if you can't talk to your partner and aim for the lower sentence. Since it is equally rational for your partner to do the same, you will both likely wind up in jail for a longer time. The Cuban Missile Crisis of 1962 put an end to these "war games" by installing a red telephone so that hostile leaders could at least talk to each other to assess motives and plans before activating a nuclear weapon, unlike the prisoners in the cells who could not communicate with each other and plan a most effective strategy for their joint gain.

The Prisoner's Dilemma operates with many different payoff schemes and incentives but it is designed to see how negotiators without the possibility of communication (or other sources of information) make offers and react to each other. Of course, it also matters if they respond simultaneously or in sequence or if they had prior agreements (an Omertà oath to "never squeal" or "defect") stronger than the current negotiation situation. The point here is that everyday negotiations present dilemmas about first offers, responses, cooperation, or defection choices. These negotiation problems come with the opportunity to gather information, including research, communication and testing, trust exercises, and verification.

Our real challenge in "mixed" situations is to see how much we can productively create and expand what is at issue (and perhaps add parties to create more resources) before we might have to develop frameworks for allocation. Consider classic labor negotiations—disputes about wages and hours became more integrative when more issues were available for trades—adding job security (and procedures for lay-offs or redundancies) and other social benefits (such as leave days, child and family care, and negotiations over work rules, supervision, governance, promotion rules, safety, and other terms and conditions of employment). Labor negotiations are often thought of as the most competitive and "zero-sum" (one dollar to the worker is one dollar away from the employer) but in fact, when there are other issues on the table a more complex menu of offers is available to negotiate. When only two issues or two parties are involved, distributive division may be inevitable, but with the addition of issues or parties, mixed models of negotiation may lead to more collective benefit. Or, in more economistic terms—more Pareto optimal utility (making each party as well off as they can be without further harm to the

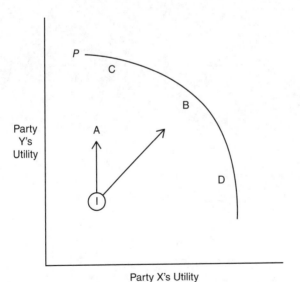

3. Pareto optimality. C, B, and D represent possible points of agreement for Parties X and Y.

others)—usually by seeking trades of differently valued items, and by recognizing the iterative aspect of these kinds of negotiation (Figure 3). Labor negotiations also reveal another important (and sometimes problematic aspect of "mixed" negotiations)—union members may not all value the same things in the same way, so constituents, especially in group settings, may have mixed desires that will have to be reconciled when dealing with the other side, what some negotiation analysts have called negotiations "behind" the table (with constituents), different from negotiations "across" the table with the "other side," who also have a "behind" the table negotiation.

Chapter 3
Contexts in negotiation

In every negotiation the parties are embedded in some culture, social grouping, identity, location, and situation which is larger than they are. Contexts vary so we cannot assume that particular conceptual models apply in all circumstances. There are distinct variables that will affect how a negotiation is framed, conducted, interpreted, and implemented. Some of those factors are structural aspects of the situation—such as the norms and conventions of a particular industry. Other variables include the people doing the negotiation—power differentials, relationships, identity. Other factors (more mutable or changeable by the parties) include such things as the mode of engagement (in person, online). This chapter explores several factors that may set the context in which any negotiation is situated. Though some negotiation scholars and practitioners have sought to describe universal processes of negotiations in different cultures, it is more likely that negotiations will have different structures and processes in different situations.

Purpose and stakes

Every negotiation starts with a purpose—what is sought to be accomplished? Is this negotiation about buying and selling—a *market-based* negotiation, often with norms and conventions specific to different markets (bargaining souks, regulated securities markets, farmers' markets, fine art auctions, commercial contracts). Conventions and norms about commodity market negotiations are as old as ancient markets. We have historical evidence of contracts written on stones and early forms of papyrus. Negotiations with considerably larger stakes include *peace treaties and agreements between nations for conflict resolution or trade.*

Most negotiations anticipate the *creation of a relationship*, whether a one-off sales agreement, a contract, a longer lasting *constitutive agreement, like a constitution or by-laws for a corporation or non-profit entity*, and so will have many future-oriented issues to consider about governance, beyond only a price. But negotiations also often involve *dissolutions*—marriages, partnerships, companies, and employment—which will often look backward to deal with or resolve past wrongs, as well as create rules of engagement for the future (e.g. child custody, severance pay, references). How one conceives of a negotiation as *future oriented* or *past dispute resolving*, or reparative or retributive, will greatly affect the frame with which we approach the other parties. Of course, it is always important to consider that one side's goals may not always be the same as the other parties' and a meta-negotiation about goals and purpose may be necessary to move forward. Parties have different motivations for seeking something from the other side (money, apology, retribution, compensation, profit, clarity about rules and governance) and so goals and purposes are also related to individual social and psychological needs and may or may not be tightly connected to more instrumental goals.

Perhaps the single most important factor in any negotiation is the "stakes" of the negotiation—what is the *res, materiel* being negotiated? Is there a single item of sale (a commodity, a piece of property, an asset, company, or stock, services) to be bought and sold at one time or with continuous relations (consider warranties for products, etc.)? Is an issue being negotiated capable of being expanded or traded for something else or even recharacterized (consider contingent payments or demilitarized zones of land). Must an item be divided eventually or not? Joint custody of children emerged in family law as a recognition that physical custody of children did not have to be awarded to only one parent, when children benefited from continuing physical presence in the divorced parents' new households, and custody itself was legally reconstituted after creative negotiations by family lawyers. New time-sharing property concepts have allowed such negotiated landownership as cooperatives, condominiums, and shared rentals. So every negotiation requires an audit of what is possible to consider outcomes that may not require division or paying all money at once.

Subject matter

Closely related to stakes is an analysis of the subject matter of the negotiation. In some matters, for example, real estate sales, mergers and acquisitions, labor negotiations (collective bargaining), international trade, environmental uses, diplomacy, and others, there will not only be some informal norms of negotiation but also formal legal rules and requirements that may restrict what negotiators can do and also may impose certain requirements on mandatory information disclosures and legally required terms. Negotiators may have to consider "the shadow of the law" in what the possible ZOPAs, BATNAs, and ATNAs can be. Negotiations used to create new entities—corporations, non-governmental organizations, or partnerships—will likely be different in many ways than those which are contested lawsuit settlement negotiations or very testy peace and diplomatic agreements (e.g. the Easter Accords in Northern Ireland and EU–Brexit negotiations). Some matters may require specialists or *negotiation agents* (lawyers, brokers, dealmakers, as in entertainment, sports, diplomacy).

Content of issues

An important factor in all negotiations is both the content and number of issues. Having more issues is often better, as more issues means more trades can be made. It is better to have more than just a price at stake. The content of issues to be considered includes such things as whether there are *short-term issues* to be resolved (what color wine we want for dinner) or *longer-term issues* (in what city we are going to live) that draw on different needs and goals of the parties. If the issues are very important (e.g. family matters, diplomatic issues, legal issues) in creating precedents, in affecting many people outside of the immediate parties (think environmental agreements and future generations), we will likely analyze the negotiation differently (who should be at the table and for how long) than if the issue is simpler and only affects a few. This time we will see my movie choice, next time you can choose (alternating agreements). Or if we are not sure what the value of the deal is or what the underlying science is, we will make a contingent agreement now and revisit what we have done when the facts have changed.

Are issues equally valued or can we trade things to which we assign different values? Are we better off disaggregating some issues (dividing them up, seeking partial agreements) or aggregating them—let's agree first on big things (e.g. let's form a partnership to create food banks to ameliorate hunger and then see what we can do about how to allocate responsibilities for acquiring food and distributing it). For example, consider Pret à Manger, the successful British sandwich purveyor which has a policy of donating unsold food at the end of the day to those in need. When Pret entered the US market, however, it was met with complex health and safety rules that, at first, did not allow unsold food to be given away. But after appealing to the altruistic policy of making otherwise fresh but unsold food available to various local governments, some municipalities then figured out new ways to further the policy (e.g. changing regulations, involving food bank middlemen, and changing taxation allocations). Pret's policy itself was an "add on" appeal for enhanced business success by adding an issue to the usual monetary negotiation of buying lunch.

Parties

The classic conception of a negotiation is two parties haggling over price either at a table or, these days, on a phone or computer, but in reality many, if not most, negotiations have more than two parties. In complex negotiations there might be principal parties, with their *agents, lawyers, brokers, or representatives*, which complicate patterns of communication, disclosures, and requirements for agreements. In many modern negotiations (where the family should go on holiday, virtually all diplomatic negotiations, business deals, and legal disputes) there will be many other parties to the negotiation (insurers, employees or employers, ex-spouses, children, allies, neighbors, etc.). *Multi-party* negotiations have their own separate logic from dyadic (two-party) negotiations: when do we know if we have agreement—do all parties have to agree or only a few?; coalition formation, vetoes and holdouts, often requiring separate consideration of ground rules of procedure for conversations, as well as decision rules for knowing if an agreement has been reached. In addition, information issues (total transparency vs selective information sharing) are far more complex with multiple parties (see Chapter 6). When the negotiators are themselves groups or organizations, rather than individuals, there will be internal negotiations before any negotiation with the other parties.

Accountability/agency/authority

Whether principal negotiators are the only ones affected by a negotiation will certainly influence how the negotiation is conducted. Diplomats are answerable to their Prime Ministers and countrymen (and the rest of the world), government officials and elected officers to their constituencies, labor negotiators to their trade unions, lawyers to their clients, corporate leaders and businesses to their shareholders and employees, parents to their children, so the range of analysis and action for any negotiator may be circumscribed by what constituencies require. Some negotiations have legal accountability built in but others may involve losing re-election if those affected by any negotiation are dissatisfied. Accountability can ensure standards are met in certain regulated areas of negotiation but it may also constrain what particularly creative and independent negotiators can accomplish. This is called the "authority" to bargain that principals give their agents and agents are usually bound by instructions given to them by those to whom they are accountable.

Visibility/publicity

What can be done in any negotiation is also greatly affected by how *public or secret* the negotiation is. Although it is often important to use confidentiality and secrecy in negotiations so that parties can share what is really important to them (for possible trading) without the whole world knowing, many argue for transparency in negotiations (especially those involving public goods or issues). President Ronald Reagan used publicity effectively (for him) by publicly announcing he would not engage in labor negotiations with the striking trade union representing government air traffic controllers in 1981. "If you don't come to work tomorrow you are fired," he said, demonstrating openly he was engaged in a hard form of bargaining to avoid acceding to demands for increased wages. It succeeded. The air traffic controllers who did not come to work were fired (close to 12,000), the trade union was broken, and many thought the President had lived up to his "tough guy" image. The risk of such public negotiations, however, is that they can backfire (if not backed up with the kind of unilateral power that President Reagan had)

40

when there is no place to move in the negotiation without "losing face." One school of negotiation championed by the former head of General Electric Inc.'s labor negotiations, General Boulware (known as "Boulwarism"), was to make one public wage offer in collective bargaining and then refuse to bargain further, announcing a "take it or leave it" policy. This strategy never caught on in labor negotiations, as cultural norms were that labor conditions should be fully negotiated, with expectations of multiple issues and trade-offs (wages, hours, and other working conditions). High risk labor, political, and diplomatic negotiations are seldom conducted in public any more. When they are, the results are often poor (see US sports collective bargaining negotiations in hockey, football, and basketball, where extreme publicly announced positions have led to impasses and cancellation of whole sports seasons).

Philosophers and political scientists often argue that transparency is a moral necessity in such important political negotiations as the creation of a constitution, but political scientist Jon Elster has argued that the American constitutional process, negotiated in secret (without public meetings or even daily reports of committees and convention-wide negotiations), was able to construct a more robust (with more secret compromises) and lasting document than the French constitution (both negotiated within a few years of each other), which was conducted with public deliberations and daily "press conferences" that forced the parties into more rigid positions from which they could not retreat, as their constituencies were watching.

Voluntary/compulsory negotiations

Are the parties seeking each other out to voluntarily conduct a negotiation to seal a deal, confirm a transaction, or settle a dispute or are they locked in a compulsory negotiation which will constrain what they are able to do? It is commonly thought that transactional negotiations are "easier" because they are more voluntary—we sit down with someone to create a deal that is good for us (and hopefully good for them too) and if not, we use our BATNA or ATNA to walk away if we don't like what is offered. Conversely, in the American criminal justice system, where most cases are settled by plea bargain (a negotiated agreement on charge or sentence by prosecutor and defense counsel) and the "going rate" of punishment for each crime is generally known, the negotiation will feel limited and mandatory.

Consider another example of "compelled" negotiations—hostage and terrorism negotiations. When hostage takers, pirates, or terrorists seize humans (or highly valued property items) and demand ransoms or other "concessions," governments, family members, and private corporations may feel compelled to negotiate. To try to discourage and disincentivize such actions, the United States has often stated a policy of "we don't negotiate with hostage takers!" The truth is the United States government has negotiated for release of hostages (Iran 1980) and corporations now often buy insurance for ransom payments for kidnapped corporate officers or property. It is not particularly credible these days to say "we NEVER negotiate," but these kinds of involuntary negotiations are particularly difficult. A great deal of expertise has now developed locally and nationally (both the New York City Police Department and the FBI have specialty units for hostage negotiations), and internationally (specialty insurance companies for piracy and kidnapping). One interesting issue for negotiation professionals is to what extent this specialized form of negotiation can teach us techniques for use in other contexts. Some hostage negotiators suggest the goals of such negotiations are totally different from other forms of negotiation (just save lives, don't solve any larger problems) while others suggest some tools may work in all contexts—just really listen to the other side (hostage taker) and find out what they really need/want (money, recognition, fame, prisoner exchange, political goals).

Timing, deadlines, and contingent negotiations

Negotiations vary in their demands for speed, finality, or their ability to be conducted over a longer time span. Many believe that firm *deadlines* are important to moving a long process to conclusion. Famously, George Mitchell, who mediated the Northern Ireland Good Friday Agreement Easter Accords (1998), after two frustrating years of cross-Atlantic negotiations, finally called a deadline by saying he was flying home at Easter to greet his newborn child and not returning (and used that fact to ask the negotiators to consider how many newborns they would save in Northern Ireland if they agreed on a peace plan, which they ultimately did).

Two important concepts in the timing of negotiations suggest that when there is a "*hurting stalemate*" and the parties can no longer stand the pain of death, injury, or loss they will finally come to the table. Hurting stalemates may sometimes be created or manipulated (in a good way) to make the parties see that a problematic situation is "*ripe*" for negotiation. Others say that disputes and transactions are not necessarily like fruit that may be ripe for only a day or two, but that there is more than one time in a negotiation that is particularly good for engaging in negotiation and perhaps settling terms. Some go even further to suggest that many negotiations (Israel–Palestine, the end of apartheid in South Africa, racial injustice) may require generations of long and complex negotiations, with many parties, and require contingent agreements that may need to be revisited as conditions change.

Lawyer negotiators know that many legal disputes and lawsuits settle on the courthouse steps because it is the deadline of trial that finally causes the parties to focus clearly on the merits of their claims and to fear the risk of a brittle (win–lose) court result. Whether such last minute negotiated settlements are wise remains unclear.

Firm deadlines in negotiations often serve as a spur to last minute concessions or compromises, but finality may have to be balanced against the quality and sustainability of a negotiated agreement, which might take more time (and cost) to be sure all issues are addressed thoughtfully.

Routineness or uniqueness of negotiation

Some negotiations are so frequent there may literally be a template for negotiating a price, returning a defective good, or obtaining customer service. A recent illustration of such negotiations is now commonly used in online dispute resolution (ODR). eBay has used ODR negotiations (for complaints, returns, and refunds) for years, now claiming to process over 60 million disputes a year. Companies like Amazon, airlines, and many consumer services now provide for quick negotiations over consumer complaints, defective products, and services by offering dialogue boxes and asynchronous negotiations with both live customer service representatives and, more efficiently now, algorithms (e.g. "if the customer spends more than $500/year and the dispute is less than $50, just refund the money claimed"). While critics worry that this form of negotiation is hardly an opportunity to create value and find optimal creative solutions, it is fast, usually cheap, and may possibly provide some feedback for the large entity on the other side of the complaints. And in an ironic twist on this form of repetitive routine negotiations, scorned customers can enhance their negotiation power by posting complaints publicly and downgrading service or product providers on social media rating sites. I have termed this process of public posting or shaming as a new form of "class action," calling it "Getting to Yelp" (Yelp is a social media site for rating restaurants, hotels, doctors, and tradesmen, among other products and services, a play on the words of "Getting to Yes"). The "routine" negotiation has been converted into a public shaming exercise that often gets quick relief (with a negotiated outcome of refund in return for removal of adverse reputational material).

At the other extreme of routine negotiations are those which are so complex and one-off (Iranian and North Korea nuclear negotiations, EU–Brexit) that there may be little one can use from conventional negotiation structures, though almost all diplomatic one-off negotiators make use of analogies and history. The key in such high stakes one-off negotiations is to learn something, but not too much, from what seems like a similar negotiation. Not every negotiation with an enemy is Chamberlain–Hitler at Munich (causing some diplomatic negotiators to be reticent to make any concessions), nor is every negotiation like the Cuban Missile Crisis of 1962 (Khrushchev's "backing down" from a strong threat issued by President Kennedy).

Power/leverage

Turning to the people doing the negotiation, we approach one of the most fraught elements of negotiation—power. How do we deal with power imbalances (countries, organizations, and individuals), when so much negotiation literature seems to assume some equality of bargaining endowments? Power means the ability to get someone else to do what you would like them to do. Leverage is the power "over" someone to get them to do what you would like, such as with threats (or actual force and violence), resource offers or withholding payments, appeals to legitimate authority (e.g. the law is on my "side," parental, employer authority), trades, or even benevolence and generosity. Critics of conventional conceptions of power have suggested that in negotiation we should think about "power with"—the ability of two or more parties to do things together they could not do alone. The negotiation itself creates power by enhancing resources, ideas, or personnel to get things done and so power is actually often particular to the negotiation itself rather than a permanent characteristic of the parties. Others suggest that power is sometimes a "perception" of power that can be altered or manipulated in many ways, such as getting others and allies to join, finding resources elsewhere, making formal process rules to avoid being taken advantage of, focusing on what value one who has "less" power can offer one with more. It is essential to analyze realistic power endowments—who really stands to gain/lose from a situation, how someone who seems to have less power (e.g. a child) creates more power (crying incessantly), what other parties are available to deal with, and, very importantly, when to walk away (if that is possible) from a situation where one might be taken advantage of.

Personal characteristics/identity/culture: gender, race, class, ethnicity, other?

In our current world much is made of who we are—our *identity*, some of it visible to others (gender, race, ethnicity, size, age, ableness, perhaps some elements of class, sometimes religion) and other parts of our identity less visible (sexual orientation, profession or occupation, sometimes religion, education, family, and social situation). How we approach these "visible" and less visible attributes in assumptions we make about others and deal with the assumptions others might make about us is an important element of modern negotiations. We can think of ourselves as presenting "outward" characteristics to others but also "inward" conceptions of ourselves (more descriptive, complex, and adjectival than based on visible stereotypes) as we imagine the characteristics of our counterparts. (I am short, no longer youthful, white, and female but I am also an expert in negotiation—how am I perceived by others; how do I present myself?) Some of these characteristics can be "managed" or manipulated and others are less mutable. Shall we all sit down to avoid size disparities, or shall we negotiate on Zoom or by email or telephone?

A vast literature in negotiation explores, inconclusively, whether women are "easy marks," less successful in competitive negotiations, or more effective problem solvers in negotiation. Though there are research studies that document many gender differences in negotiation outcomes and styles of negotiation, most of these studies have been conducted in laboratory settings (in business schools or university psychology departments). One recent study demonstrated that men in a prominent American business school became more aggressive in simulated negotiations after Donald Trump's election, but in fact achieved worse outcomes than women in the same program. Women are advised to ignore assumptions about women's so called "weakness" in competitive negotiation, to use their better problem-solving and collaborative skills, or to employ a variety of "moves and turns" to deal with both explicit bias and more subtle implicit sexism in negotiation settings. Research has demonstrated that, like so many of these identity factors, situations may matter more— professional women (lawyers, politicians, brokers) who act on behalf of others and not just themselves are no different than men in similar roles; education and professional role (leader, judge, physician, scientist) supplant gender as salient characteristics. Yet the "stereotype bind" continues to exist for many who are perceived to be "different" from assumed modal negotiators (middle-aged white males).

Everything noted about gender is even more problematic when applied to race, ethnicity, and class in many negotiations. Rigorous research (using different races of negotiators as possible purchasers of the same vehicle) has demonstrated that black men and women are offered higher prices in automobile purchases by auto dealers and even in online negotiations and purchases (e.g. Uber taxis, Airbnb residence stays) where differential prices are offered based on pictures or names of purchasers of goods or services. Many assumptions made about the financial status or extent of negotiation experience are often products of stereotypical thinking and can cause great harm to both those who make the assumptions and those who are victims of such thinking. Yet it remains a challenge to know what to do when one thinks such assumptions are in play (confront, deflect, ignore, or use agents and co-negotiators where possible).

A vast literature also suggests that "one can negotiate anything anywhere with anyone" if one masters a complex set of cultural differences in negotiation, with claimed strategies for dealing with indirect cultures (Scandinavian, Asian), hierarchical vs lateral cultures (Asian vs US), formal (German, Japanese) vs informal (US), cultures that require gifts for exchange or development of long relationships and trust (*guanxi* in China) before anything instrumental can be accomplished. Advice manuals report on differences in understanding deadlines and timing, authority, consensus, when an agreement is truly an agreement, when direct requests for information will be honored or not. On the one hand it is essential and always part of any good preparation to learn as much about one's counterpart as possible, including nationality, culture, and education. On the other hand, in our globalized world no one individual negotiator is likely to conform completely to such cultural stereotypes, especially with more hybridized educational backgrounds, migration patterns, different professions, and different negotiation situations, all of which may modify any static conception of culture. Acting on cultural assumptions by making assumptions about appropriate physical space, touching, and chains of authority is risky. In the modern world negotiators must be very careful in realizing that often negotiators speak several languages and may be able to understand what some might think is private and confidential.

If you are reading this book you are becoming part of a growing international culture that is becoming better versed in negotiation concepts and behaviors and so it might be that the "international negotiation culture" is a more salient "culture" in any negotiation than other particular cultures.

Personal characteristics/personality

Whatever the situation, people are people and one issue in any interaction is how we relate to others. Do we have a "default" personality and how will our personality interact with our counterparts? A series of psychological studies have sought to determine how we interact with others in conflictual situations. The Thomas–Kilmann Mode test (from organizational development) divides people into five modes of behavior—competitors, cooperators (or accommodators), compromisers, avoiders, and collaborators on a scale of emphasizing concern for self (assertiveness) or other (responsiveness/empathy) (Figure 4).

While it is always essential to know oneself and to consider what one might do in any situation, as well as try to learn as much as possible about one's counterpart, it is also likely that situations themselves bring forth different behaviors in each of us. Thus, it is probably not helpful to think of oneself or one's counterpart as

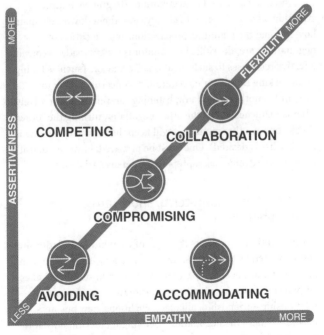

4. **Modes of behavior.**

always being competitive or cooperative, though many negotiation experts tend to frame it that way.

Although Roger Fisher and William Ury urged negotiators to "separate the people from the problem" to focus on the substance of any negotiation, it is often true that the people *are* the problem and we will need to deal with difficult people, emotions, and problematic personalities. There is a growing literature on dealing with emotions and "having difficult conversations" in negotiations that helps negotiators deal with differences in facts, preferences, values, identities, assignment of blame, and emotions. Consider how Nikita Khrushchev negotiated during the Cold War by literally banging his shoe on the podium at the United Nations, demonstrating that displays of anger, disagreement, and hostility can, and often are, used in negotiations (to grab leverage, attention, assert power, or to simply close them down). No matter how rational the planning, preparation, and execution of negotiations are, the skilled negotiator is always ready to consider effective responses to such "irrational" behaviors (such as taking a break, asking calmly for elaboration of concerns, asking to substitute another negotiator, listening carefully and attentively to what is really needed by the other negotiator, turning the "other cheek," or any other tactic that will keep the negotiation going if that is what is desired). One must be prepared, however, to walk away or, in extreme cases, prepare for defense, trial, or war.

Relationships—long-term, short-term, or in-between

Every negotiation presents the issue of what kind of relationship is contemplated by the parties. Are they in a long-term relationship already (family, business partners, vendors and suppliers, allies, employer–employee) or are they considering a long-term relationship—friendship, alliances, coalitions, new business partner—where the negotiation itself might determine what the relationship will be. Is the negotiation truly a one-off, buyer–seller situation, a compelled relationship, one of competition or enmity, not likely to be transformed. Consider those relationships that exist within the interstices of these temporal variations—divorcing couples who might want to be totally apart but who have to continue to care for children together, partners dissolving a business over time, start-up businesses that may or may not work. What kinds of risks, warranties, guarantees, and relationship terms can be made part of negotiations where the relationship itself is a negotiable item and may be subject to change as the negotiation progresses?

Medium of negotiation: face to face or online? Synchronous or asynchronous?

We tend to think of negotiators as sitting at a table facing each other, what we now call *face to face* or *person to person* (P2P) and so we think of simultaneous, synchronous communications which are conducted, interpreted, and responded to. In the more modern era of communication technology, globalization, negotiations over many time zones, and pandemic-based homework and isolation, more and more negotiations are conducted through technology which may be synchronous or asynchronous—by email, electronic contracting, and customer service. The mode or medium of negotiation itself has become a major factor in how negotiations are conducted. ODR is widely touted as allowing more access to justice as disputants (ordinary citizens with each other or consumers with complaints against government or corporate entities) can access complaint forms, make demands and arguments, and also get information and have time to think before responding.

Modern technology allows some ease of negotiation (sparing travel costs, not requiring total mobility, allowing access to many sources of information), but also may hinder access for others (those not online, some disability or accessibility issues, and computer literacy generally). However, the powerful (major corporations and government agencies) can use such technology to aggregate negotiations and decide things by algorithm, making negotiations and decisions more efficient for them, but rigid and not individualized for others. What is online agreement or justice?

Even in more conventional negotiation settings, how the negotiations are conducted is an important factor to consider—in an office—whose, yours or mine?, in a retreat setting, with room for separate (caucus) sessions if there are multiple parties, with food or not, liquor or not (think cultural differences), formal or not? Who has a seat at the table (stakeholders) and who may speak when (ground rules or free form?), will there be written records of communications, who will be the scribes and recorders? There are no easy prescriptions that if one does x, y effect will follow, but negotiators who do not consider these issues may be bested by those who do think about and plan for them.

Alternatives to negotiation

Finally, what are all my alternatives in this situation? Do I have to negotiate with this party? Where else could I go to achieve my goals? What are my "best" alternatives, beyond what I am doing here, what is the worst that could happen to me if I stay here, and what is the worst thing that could happen if I don't stay here and negotiate. Must I negotiate now or will there be a better time, or other parties with whom to negotiate later? If not negotiation and possible agreement now, then what?

Chapter 4
Behavioral choices in negotiation: What to do and why

Choosing behavior: Frameworks, contexts, and purpose

Having analyzed what a negotiation is about, it is time to come to the table (or the computer or phone) and act. This chapter explores the strategies, tactics, and skills of behavioral choices in negotiation by focusing on the stages of most negotiations, presents issues of behavioral choices within the situational differences we have explored earlier, and identifies ways to think strategically and responsively to classic negotiation dilemmas, including the power plays and nasty tactics of the bullying school of negotiation. Contexts, parties, and situations can produce different modes of behavior. All behavioral processes in negotiation are ultimately dynamic and relational—we choose to do something, "they" choose to do something, and then we react. In negotiation behavior it is useful to remember that we should never say never and never say always. The Appendix provides a useful tool—a planning document—to assist all negotiators in considering and "scripting" different moves in any negotiation.

There are three important stages to consider in any negotiation: planning "pre-negotiation" (before), conducting the negotiation (during), and executing the agreement (after). Not all negotiations move smoothly in this temporal sequence but thinking of these stages is useful for planning.

Pre-negotiation: planning

Goals, purposes—What do I want, what do they want? This can change when we actually encounter and communicate with the other parties. If we are a negotiation agent, like a lawyer or broker, we start with an *interview* of our principal—"what do you want," or "what outcome would you like to see?" This question usefully has people in negotiation consider the end states they are trying to achieve and encourages us to begin to think of alternatives. It has some danger of promising too much (sometimes I add the qualifier, "in an ideal world" what outcome would you like to see?) but at least it begins the thinking about ideal states, goals, and values and creates a benchmark to be created for evaluation of all proposals. Setting goals helps identify the appropriate framework (distributive problem—I want money, revenge, profit maximization, or possible collaborative and more integrative ideas of value creation, sharing, or more mixed approaches).

It is essential to remember that negotiation always involves another party—what do they want? In my classes I often start by asking students to negotiate some of the course requirements with me. They always focus on what they want (less written work, higher grades, fewer assignments) and frame their offers and arguments in terms of what is good for them. It is the rare student who asks, "What would you like, professor?" This signals one of the most important lessons in negotiation—think about the other side; every negotiator has to consider what the other side wants. The clever students say it will be less work for me if I have to grade fewer assignments.

Research—What do we need to know about the context of our negotiation? What are the industry norms, legal issues, facts about the other parties, other possible deals or outcomes we could explore? What more do we need to know about ourselves and our own situation? Consider the analogy of visiting the doctor—first we have a physical exam and answer questions about how we feel and where it hurts, and then the doctor may request some tests—blood, X-rays, or other advanced imaging to shed more light on what the "problem" might be—and will only then consider what treatments or solutions might work. Similarly, we do research to learn what is involved in a negotiable situation and then to consider what could be. What options are available? What legal remedies are possible, or what transactions are possible?

Crafting/creating possible solutions—Even before we talk to the other side, we begin to brainstorm with ourselves, creating and imagining various outcomes that might be possible, beginning to "frame" what we want, what we think they might want, and to ask what information we will need from all the other parties, and then to consider options and ways to make those outcomes appealing to our counterparts.

Process planning and design—We should think in advance about how we will conduct our negotiation—in person, other media, how many parties, shape of "the table," whose office or location, formal or informal settings, rules of engagement, for example ground rules about confidentiality, dealings with the media (if this is a national or international negotiation requiring accountability or transparency), minutes, recording, duration and numbers of sessions, agenda planning.

Scripting—Distinguishing strategy (overall plan for accomplishing a desired goal) from tactics (the behaviors used to get there) involves imagining as much as possible about what might happen during the negotiation. The Negotiation Plan (Appendix) and Table 2 can help us to visualize and plan for being at the table and to think in advance what we will say, what the other parties might say or do, and to consider what responses or countermoves we might make. Scripting helps planning, but flexibility, discretion, and judgment for adaptation will almost always be required. Things seldom go exactly as planned, but without a plan we may have no idea where things will go.

Table 2. Stages and phases of a negotiation by framework

I. Pre-negotiation: planning

Interview self or client—what are goals, objectives, purposes, interests, needs

Analyze—what is at stake? Materiel? Parties? (Contexts—Chapter 2)

Research—what information do I need to have? Facts, industry, other parties, law, "comparables"

What do I want to be the end state? How am I hoping this will all turn out—planning outcomes and goals, specifically—crafting and planning possible solutions

Design—site of negotiation—in person, online, who present, shape of the table, business or retreat setting, ground rules, scripting, noting tensions of planning and flexibility

II. Conducting the negotiation: During—"at the table"

Introduction—who are we? How do we identify/see each other? "foreplay"

Agenda setting—issues and process rules

Information Exchange

Conventional-distributive	Integrative/problem solving
First offer/demand	Proposals/packages
Bargaining/concessions	Brainstorming, trading
Tactics—arguments, deflection	Questions, information sharing
Manipulation	Listening, curiosity, principles
Persuasion—speaking	Responses/countermoves
Adversarial ploys/tricks	Empathy
Finding ZOPA-narrowing issues	Creating solutions and outcomes
Reaching agreement	Agreements—contingent?

III. Post-agreement—implementation and follow-through

Confirm agreement terms—draft agreement

Share agreement drafting

Specify terms of execution—payment terms, timing contingency planning

Dispute resolution clause

Evaluation—what have I learned?

Follow-up; performance, relationship

Conducting negotiations—during the negotiation

"Foreplay" and introductions—The first encounter with our counterparts is important. Who are we? Who are they? This can set the table for perceptions of or manipulation of power differentials, cultural differences, physical attributes, demographics, and professional or employment status. Names, titles, clothes, and seating are all non-substantive issues that might affect actual engagement. Seemingly innocent openings or introductions can be very significant—social distance, handshakes, nods, bows, hugs, kisses, self-descriptions, or attributed ones. Will the negotiators see themselves as equals or dominators? Will a tone of collaboration or competition be set in the first words? What roles or statuses do the negotiators occupy? I call this the "foreplay" of negotiation—what do we learn in those first encounters? Is it friendly, offering refreshments, serious curiosity, or set up to dominate? Consider the Charlie Chaplin movie *The Great Dictator* (1940) and the parodic Hitler character's use of furniture to make the Mussolini character feel even smaller than he was. Just as significant, offers, proposals, arguments, and concessions should be carefully planned and considered before the negotiation, as should presentation of self and inquiry about the other.

Agenda setting—Productive negotiations at almost any level are best served by the development of explicit agenda items *at the*

beginning. Since almost no negotiation is only about price, consider in advance what else could be at stake in the negotiation—timing and method of payments, delivery costs, quantity and quality, risk/insurance allocations, warranties, and guarantees. What are all the issues with which each party is concerned? To the extent possible, specification in advance can prevent one very dangerous negotiation tactic ("nibbling," "low balling," or backtracking) when, after agreement occurs, one party says, "oh and another thing, we cannot agree unless we also have …". This takes advantage of the assumption that with the sunk costs of the negotiation process and the commitment to the agreement made, one party can force yet another concession at the last minute to preserve the agreement. It is safe to say, in almost any negotiation, "we will not have a final agreement until we are agreed on the whole deal." Since most negotiations involve multiple issues, there are likely to be important issues of *linkage* and so one should be careful that although there might be sequential agreements on particular issues, no one issue should be considered finally decided until all issues on the agenda are addressed. As new information may be learned during the process, agendas may have to be modified, but this should be done explicitly and with the acknowledgment of all the parties.

Information exchange—How explicit should we be about our search for information? Parties can agree to exchange documents, information, ideas, proposals, potential clauses in advance (as happens in litigation during the discovery stage before a trial, or a proposed "deal sheet" in transactional negotiations) or they can engage in ad hoc use of questions during the negotiation (which can be honest or manipulative). In general, it is useful to think through what information one needs from oneself, the other parties, or people outside of the negotiation before an actual negotiation session, but it may also be useful to have a specified session which is devoted to information exchange so that the information can be processed, interpreted, and verified.

Information in negotiations can consist of *facts* about the parties, the industry or context of the negotiation, the *preferences* of the parties, including *valuations* placed on particular items and *predictions or opinions* about values and outcomes (e.g. assessment of trial outcomes in lawsuits or potential profits in transactions). It is important to have a strategy about information, a "calculus" of informational disclosures and risks. Some information must be revealed to the other parties by law (e.g. conditions of property, financial information in securities or mergers and acquisitions, truthful representations to avoid voiding of contracts for fraud). Some information is available in the public domain and thus dangerous to withhold. Much information is available on the internet, including the value of property, for example "comparables," past legal cases, corporate financial information, news reports, reputational ratings of people and businesses, and even some private information as people disclose more and more about themselves on social media. Some information may become available through legal subpoenas or private detection or disclosed by other parties (such as those who have dealt with negotiation partners before). If there is an explicit agreement to share information a strong pull of reciprocation in most negotiations should require parties to think about what they want to know about the others as they carefully consider what to reveal about themselves. The relationship of the parties is particularly important. In negotiating to create a new entity, business partnership, or marriage, consider how important it is to share honest information both about advantages of coming together but also about potential risks. It might even be important to reveal some damaging information in a negotiation to characterize and explain it and to prevent others from using it against you.

In asking for and receiving information it is important to know whether that information is trustworthy so it might be useful to "plant a trust land mine" by asking questions to which you already know the answer (but the other party does not know you know).

Sometimes this is best done with a very open-ended question—
"Can you tell me about…"—and sometimes with a very direct,
closed question (seeking exact confirmation or disconfirmation).
All of the traditional journalists' questions are useful here. Using
Who? What? Where? When? Why? and How? questions about
elements of the situation and parties helps to identify what is truly
important and what is being shared honestly. If parties in a
negotiation are to develop good agreements they must know
whether the information they are sharing with each other is
trustworthy. This test of asking questions to which one knows the
answers already is not foolproof. One good or bad answer may not
accurately inform about the other party's total information base,
but it is one way to begin to assess the trustworthiness of one's
counterparts. Skillful negotiators know how to deflect or avoid
such inquiries, often by asking their own questions, answering
partially, or answering another (unasked) question, rather than
answering, so persistence and recording of important inquiries is
essential to obtain as much information as needed. Facts,
information, and even negotiation preferences may change during
any negotiation, so it is useful to constantly revisit information
exchanges for updates (some will be required by law).

First offers/demands/proposals/packages—This is an area of
great conflict in the field. There are those who say, "always make
the first offer, go high, use your highest aspirations to *anchor* the
numbers, values and arguments and grab as much of the
negotiable space as possible." There is some research to support
the notion that people who make high first offers or demands tend
to capture more of what they ask for. But it is also true that very
high demands can lead to impasses and walkouts by the other
side. Others suggest that it is often better to let the other party go
first as a way of learning what they value and to encourage them
to say as much as possible about *why*. The first offer from the
other party is an opportunity for information, as long as one is
careful about not letting the anchor value hang in the air too long
or without response. It is important to think carefully about

framing first proposals, offers, or packages—you, too, are giving information about what you value when you say your first piece in a negotiation; the other side will be listening and learning too.

Conventional, distributive one-issue negotiations might be structured with offers and demands, made sequentially and with responses and concessions, but in other contexts it is better to think about presenting proposals (with many issues combined) or packages of proposals, as in labor negotiations and international trade and diplomacy, combining a set of desired items to be discussed so that a stage is set for trades, opportunities to create value, and new proposals, and an ability to begin to measure, in multi-issue settings, what the varied trade-offs might be with respect to different issues. Here is a place to see the initial value of short-term issues vs longer-term issues (e.g. do we care more about hourly wages now or protections against lay-offs or access to health care in the future?).

Bargaining, movement, brainstorming—This is what most people think of as the heart of any negotiation process—how we move from offers, proposals, and packages to agreement. Despite many efforts to describe simple rules of efficiency or profit maximization, behaviors in this stage of negotiation are highly dependent on the goals, materiel of the negotiation, and the parties. In a conventional distributive, single-issue negotiation parties make offers/demands and concessions on a linear scale until they arrive at a settlement point (which often is the midpoint between the first two opening offers). But as the parties engage in what is called the "negotiation dance" to argue and persuade about their demands, they will ultimately concede in order to reach agreement.

Many negotiators randomly propose numbers and come down as negotiation conversation proceeds, but research into negotiation behavior suggests that having a reason behind any number is a better way to anchor one's desired numbers and prevent slippage or making undesired concessions. Similarly, asking the other party for the principles behind their proffered numbers may expose offers as purely arbitrary. Reasons for offers should be related to the value in the case. Consider this real-world negotiation at an antiques market:

BUYER: How much is that beautiful antique ring?
SELLER: Two hundred dollars.
BUYER: Sorry, I only have 50 dollars with me.
(A common buyer's ploy is to announce a limited budget available— may not work so well in non-cash settings)
SELLER: But you drove here and had to pay at least 75 dollars to fill your gas tank. Isn't this lasting piece of jewelry worth more than one tank of gas? (Attempting to use an anchor value of the amount of fuel needed to drive to the market.)
BUYER: Oh, great, if you will take the price of a single tank of gas, I can tell you I drive a mini which gets really good mileage and it only cost me 40 dollars to fill the tank. Using your argument, I'll take the ring for $40.00!

Seller is now hoist on his own petard—using a "reason" for a number; that "reason" had nothing to do with the actual value of the ring and has now become the price of the ring! So, have reasons for offers, demands, and numbers, but they should be tied to the subject matter of the negotiation.

In such conventional offer–response negotiations it is useful to analyze concession patterns. When concession patterns come in predictable units (e.g. 25 cents/hour for wages, $100,000 in major deals) it is easier to analyze where the other side is going. Research demonstrates that as concessions get smaller you can assume you are getting closer to your counterpart's reservation price (or bottom line). For that reason, some negotiation analysts suggest making concessions or moves which are asymptotic (odd and different numbers, e.g. 23 cents, rather than 20 or 25) so that one's goals and bottom lines are not so obvious (assuming one is in a negotiation where one prefers not to reveal where one is headed).

The "movement" process is somewhat different in an integrative negotiation—instead of single demands and responses, negotiators spend time sharing information and then either presenting more than one proposal or a package of suggestions in a multi-issue negotiation or using a *brainstorming* process to come up with proposals together. The brainstorming process, originally derived from creativity and group decision-making exercises in advertising, involves people coming up with as many ideas to solve a problem ("storm the problem") as possible without initial evaluation or critique of those ideas (and including wild and possibly implausible ideas) and then later combining, improving, modifying, and finally choosing some of those ideas.

There are now many processes of "choosing," from voting to anonymous posting with sticky notes in different colors used to rate desirability of particular options, or using flip charts and other "tools" to move things around. In the entertainment world, a version of this technique is called "storyboarding"—picking themes, issues, and characters and then using moving pieces to create "arcs" of stories (or clauses in a document or scenes in a screenplay or elements of a deal) to examine various possibilities. Many of these techniques (and others, like "free-writing" or now "crowdsourcing" in more electronic and even anonymous settings) are used when skilled facilitators are brought into negotiation and decision-making situations. This process depends on some trust being established by the parties and tends to have a more creative, "lighter" atmosphere than conventional adversarial and competitive bargaining. The key is that nothing is agreed to until all is agreed to and the hope is that new possibilities will be visualized from the interactive process itself.

Another form of "movement" process is the creation of a "one-text" document that contains clauses submitted by all parties which are shared and commented on (with trades, re-drafts, critiques, new proposals, and time-outs). This process was used in the successful Camp David Peace Accords, mediated by President Jimmy Carter in 1978. Those peace negotiations operated with very little face-to-face time. Anwar Sadat and Menachem Begin had many difficult issues between them (political, national, and personal) and separate caucus meetings, steered by aides, representatives, and third-party mediators, were used effectively to "expand" the processes and techniques used to achieve a complex peace agreement for Egypt and Israel (with the financial and military support and third-party insurance provided by the US). (Remember it is sometimes very helpful to add issues (for trades) and add parties (for resources, ideas, and insurance).)

When the issues are complex and multiple, single-offer/concession arguments are less likely to be successful. Such negotiations often depend on trades, rather than concessions, and there will often be *linkage*—how each term is agreed to depends on what happens to the rest of the package. When issues are complex or facts are not totally known, the more integrative process permits contingent agreements to be re-evaluated when facts or needs change.

The more mixed framework described in Chapter 2 (creating and claiming value) will share elements of these models, often in reverse. The parties will spend time brainstorming, creating value, exploring many new options, but then will have to choose particular outcomes. The inevitable claiming or dividing up value or items should still be conducted with rationales, but with some better trust mechanisms and relationship building that emerge from the more creative parts of the process.

Tactics, moves, and turns—When we turn to the tactics employed by negotiators (whether in service to maximizing gain and distributive outcomes or seeking creative solutions) one should always ask *why* am I (or "they") doing this? What is this behavioral choice accomplishing in the negotiation? How is each action helping to achieve the ultimate goal? Here we look at some common tools, techniques, moves, ploys, and tricks that may appear in any negotiation and how we can respond to some moves that are problematic, or even sneaky. It may be useful to separate different conceptual moves (such as reframing, aggregating, or disaggregating issues) from those which are simply behavioral (e.g. deflecting answering difficult questions).

The first move in any negotiation may signal what mindset the negotiator is using. Employing a computerized form of the Prisoner's Dilemma (described in Chapter 2) political scientist Robert Axelrod asked scholars in several fields to program interactions with all others in a "Prisoner's Dilemma tournament." Each participant wrote a set of instructions about whether to "cooperate" or "defect" when meeting another player. The winner, Anatol Rapoport, a Canadian mathematician, produced a program that did "better" than all other submissions, now known as the "tit for tat" strategy. When dealing with another (without any prior communication), the program began first by cooperating, then defecting when defected against, then being forgiving (defecting for only one round) in the hope of "teaching" the other side to cooperate too. Axelrod suggests the lessons are: be nice, don't be envious, don't be the first to defect, reciprocate cooperation (and defection) but don't be too clever (trying to outrun the other side). The tournament has been repeated many times and although in subsequent iterations a few other programs have come close to or "won" a round against Tit for Tat, it remains a good strategy for many kinds of negotiations—international diplomacy, trade, situations where one does not know the other party, business and legal negotiations. Related research has demonstrated that it is far easier to escalate a dispute than to de-escalate so it makes sense (in most cases) to begin seeking collaboration (being "nice" in Axelrod's terms) and then to escalate or "defect" (but not for too long if impasse, stalemate, or war will result) as necessary.

Those who begin with high first offers (signaling perhaps a desire to negotiate conventionally) or use classic power or hard bargaining tactics (monopolizing space and talking time, using threats, refusing to answer questions or reveal information, using deception or exaggeration ("bluffing and puffing"), making demands or take it or leave it offers, using strong persuasion without really listening to other arguments, pushing false deadlines, adding issues after agreements (low balling and nibbling), using intimidation, insults, and personal attacks, or even totally irrational behaviors (walking out, tossing papers, or banging shoes on the table), outnumbering the other side, using the "good cop/bad cop" strategy to confuse who has authority and to threaten, refusing to reciprocate offers or concessions, or just being plain stubborn) present dilemmas of response for those who want to negotiate more effectively.

So what do we do when these unpleasant tactics are used against us? Fortunately, for every "power play" there are now a variety of countermoves and suggestions about how to change the game or monitor one's own reactions, supported by social psychological research. Most important is the choice whether to explicitly confront these tactics by asking, "and what do you think x or y is actually accomplishing here?" Making explicit what a negotiator on the other side hopes will implicitly make you feel weak and then concede often deflates the desired effect of such behavior.

Negotiation scholar Deborah Kolb has labeled the responses to these tactics "moves and turns"—ways of countering, challenging, or changing the efforts to use "social positioning" to employ domination techniques in negotiation. When negotiators meet they are the products of the social structures from which they come (professional, educational, generational, gender, racial, ethnic, class, and organizational background) as they meet as individuals to accomplish goals for themselves as well as those they represent. Thus, it is always important to ask, is this about me (the negotiator) or what the parties are trying to do?—that is, return the focus to the substance of the negotiation. Kolb suggests some strategies for dealing with these efforts at social domination at the bargaining table: (1) interrupting; (2) questioning (what do you think you are accomplishing here?); (3) correcting; (4) ignoring; or (5) diverting (rather than dealing directly with the offending tactic, reframing to focus on the issues at hand, or asking the other party a question to make them respond to you).

In literature exploring discrimination and power imbalances in negotiation, others suggest such tactics as (1) becoming a team yourself (empower by adding others to the negotiation team); (2) switching counterparts where possible (asking for another negotiator, moving up the supervisory or managerial chain, especially recommended for online negotiations); (3) using silence; (4) taking a break to disrupt the unproductive dynamics; or (5) where possible, using active listening, questioning, empathy, and real human communication to literally transform the encounter by exploring real motives and interests and breaking down the conventions of traditional negotiations. Finally, by presenting solutions or options that are good for the other party (as Larry Susskind suggests, "write their victory speech"), as well as one's own, one can sometimes transcend a bad process to achieve a good outcome. (Without the drama of *The Godfather* one can make the other party "an offer they can't refuse," not because of a threat but because it is too good for them to turn down.)

Reaching agreements—As any successful negotiation seems to end with an agreement, it is essential to confirm terms, promises, and mutual obligations. After a tense time of negotiating it is common for people to sigh with relief when it is over and walk away. Many a negotiation later fails when terms are left ambiguous or there is a lack of clarity about who will do what when. Especially thorny when legal disputes are settled through negotiation is what are the terms of "release" (against further legal liability). All of this must also be negotiated (including exact language) if the negotiation is to be truly completed.

Post-agreement: Implementation—after the negotiation

Confirm terms of agreement and agreement drafting responsibilities—When negotiators leave the negotiation table it is important to be sure everyone knows what they are expected to do and when. Diplomatic negotiations often use studied ambiguities to make agreements and avoid conflict, and language differences may introduce different interpretations of the same word. Many international organizations and the EU put major documents in many languages, sometimes causing more disputes about meaning later and sometimes requiring interpretation by another authoritative source such as a court or tribunal. This is often true for negotiated legislation as well. Legislators agree on general terms of what a statute is attempting to do, but specifics of regulation or enforcement may not be well described. National constitutions vary enormously in how they were negotiated to declare basic values, rights, and governmental structures vaguely or with great detail (compare the generally vague US constitution to the detailed South African) and the United Kingdom and Israel have never committed to a single written constitutional document, leaving interpretation of governmental obligations and citizen rights to courts to interpret. Unfortunately, the same may be true in ordinary contracts, although not always done deliberately. Law reports are full of cases where courts have been called upon to interpret what was meant by particular terms of use, such as warranties (for what?), indemnification (for what?). Terms of art in particular industries may be different in others, for example FOB = "free on board" (seller pays for delivery costs). Parties to negotiation should try to specify what they want to be clear about and what they want to leave ambiguous or contingent for future consideration. Not being clear in agreements can ignite post-negotiation disputes.

Who drafts the agreement is similarly very important. While many negotiation advice books suggest that one should "grab the pen" (or keyboard) and take control of the drafting of final agreements to maintain control of the language, obligations, and responsibilities, this is in fact a dangerous strategy. In many legal systems (including the Anglo-American common law), if there is a dispute about the contract language, courts, as a matter of rules of contract interpretation, will interpret the terms *against the drafter*. Thus, to ensure clarity and maximum enforceability it is best to share drafting and to be clear that all parties have participated in memorializing the final agreement. In many complex negotiations, there may be a "deal sheet" or a Memorandum of Understanding (MOU) that precedes formal contracting. Such documents should be signed, redlined (commented on), or initialed by all parties to demonstrate agreement and participation in the agreed-to terms. In complex negotiations this is the time to engage professionals (lawyers, solicitors, career diplomats) if they have not yet been present to assure agreements meet formal requirements of law and custom.

Terms of performance and execution—It is important to specify who will do what when and how performance will be assured or measured. Will there be risk insurance for unforeseen circumstances (weather, pandemics, delays, illness, title and ownership defects), guarantees, and warranties? If payments are to be made—how and by what dates: electronic transfer, cash, stocks and bonds, bartered items, and is there a need for an escrow account to be established before payment changes hands (e.g. while a property is inspected or a product or service is completed to satisfaction or completion assurance accounts in construction and the entertainment world)? If the agreement provides for some contingent agreements (if x, then y...) the conditions for revisiting terms should be made clear. Contingent agreements are common in some financial settings, political negotiations, and increasingly in environmental agreements as monitoring of air or water quality (often by a third party) or the effects of some land use (pollution) may trigger a renegotiation of set standards or obligations.

***Dispute resolution provisions*—**Knowing that many negotiations leave ambiguities unresolved or that new circumstances may occur that will produce disagreements about what a negotiated agreement means, a good negotiation agreement provides a mechanism for resolving such disputes before the parties initiate litigation, war, or other unproductive acts. The simplest form of dispute resolution is just to provide for "renegotiation" of any disputes that arise, requiring parties to come back to the negotiation table before instigating a lawsuit (what is called a *condition precedent* before allowing formal litigation about the matter). Sometimes in more complex arrangements and, increasingly, in international treaties, there will be a "tier" or menu of dispute resolution options, starting with renegotiation by the parties, mediation by a third party, and then non-binding or binding (final) arbitration by a third party (not a judge or a court but a decision maker chosen by the parties).

Negotiation is now part of a larger field "A" (alternative, appropriate, accessible) DR (dispute resolution), *ADR*, which encourages people to find a process of engagement that fits the context and substance of their matter, what is called "fitting the forum to the fuss." A good negotiated agreement should provide for consideration of what to do if something goes wrong.

Evaluation*—*what have we learned? When a negotiation is "over" parties should debrief and troubleshoot their agreement. What did we do well? What might we have done differently? What might go wrong with this agreement that perhaps we should do something about now, before a new dispute arises. If the negotiation involves an ongoing relationship it will be useful to debrief and to "debug" the negotiation together. In an organizational or client setting a good negotiator asks for feedback from anyone who was part of the negotiation or within the organization with some expertise about what might/should have happened. Negotiators make contracts, deals, treaties, laws, and relationships that affect others. Finding out what they think about what was accomplished is an important part of the negotiation process. We should learn something from every negotiation we do, but also not learn too much. Negotiation theory and practice is full of false analogies—don't be Chamberlain at Munich and give in too easily (encouraging more competitive behavior in places where it might not be appropriate). It is much easier to escalate a situation than to de-escalate so it is often better to start at least with efforts to agree (as Chamberlain did at Munich and John Kennedy did in the Cuban Missile Crisis, after delivering a strong public threat). The good negotiator learns from every event but also knows to always analyze the context and situation. Ironically, in general, very few generalizations about negotiation are universal.

Chapter 5
Challenges to reaching negotiated agreements

Despite all good intentions, many negotiations fail. Sometimes this is because there is no Zone of Possible Agreement—the parties' needs, preferences, and goals do not overlap. A large body of research in psychology, sociology, and behavioral economics documents that we often don't reach agreements when we could, because of human "error" in information processing, data errors, explicit and implicit biases, and human psychological and social reactions, which can lead to less-than-optimal behavioral choices. This chapter explores these human reactions to others and information that inhibit good negotiation choices and offers some correctives for better negotiated results.

While many cognitive scientists call these processes "errors" or deviance from "rational" thinking, I prefer to think of this as more descriptive of human behavior (we all do these things) rather than prescriptive. There are different processes in decision making including the "rational" (good reasons), the "irrational" (bad reasons), and the "arational" (without reason, but perhaps drawing on other systems or values, e.g. emotional, political, cultural, or ethical). What is "rational" in a particular negotiation depends on the parties' needs and values.

Research into human behavior also documents "multiple intelligences," including quantitative-logical, linguistic, emotional-interpersonal and intra-personal, kinesthetic-body, spatial, naturalistic, musical, and moral and, more controversially, spiritual and existential. Negotiation draws on many of these different forms of intelligence, some of which are more likely to help with creativity, problem solving, and as correctives to some of the challenges described here.

Cognitive "errors"

A new body of cognitive and social psychology research demonstrates how humans sometimes make ill-informed decisions. This work is well summarized in the work of Daniel Kahneman and Amos Tversky (and others) who describe two systems of thought: "thinking fast and slow." In *System I* thinking (fast thinking) we use shortcuts in our decision making ("heuristics") to act quickly and *automatically* or *intuitively*, based on what we think we know (sometimes using stereotypes and categories and sometimes incorrect use of data which are readily called up in our brains). In *System II* thinking (slow) we are more likely to do research and exercise deliberative thought processes before we act. Knowing when to use fast or slow thinking processes in negotiation is very important. We need slow, deliberative thinking when we plan for negotiations and consider how and when to make offers and in the creation of contingent solutions in complex situations; too often we act on the faster, automatic processes, especially when responding in the moment to what others do.

Framing-anchoring

The first major issue in any negotiation is *who frames* the issues, the problem to be solved, and *what words (or numbers)* are used to characterize the negotiation. Is the negotiation a one-issue (price) sales issue or are there other issues to be addressed? Who are the relevant parties? The first statement, offer, or number can anchor the parameters and tone of the entire negotiation.

Scarcity bias

Most negotiators think they are bargaining over something which is zero-sum (or a "fixed pie" mentality)—a dollar for me is one less for you. This framing is one of the most common and dangerous cognitive errors we can make. It causes us to adopt a mindset that begins with distributive bargaining assumptions, which in turn leads to competitive behaviors such as a reluctance to share information. This bias often assumes that all parties value the same things equally (e.g. money) and so will have to compete over maximization of those values. This is also a dangerous assumption as non-competitive, complementary needs can permit more trades (money too often becomes the proxy for a more varied set of issues). Remember it is almost always easier to escalate (to move to competitive non-sharing modes) if you must than to do the reverse—de-escalate. In order to look for more options and creative solutions it is better to start with framing that welcomes, rather than forecloses, information, ideas, and suggestions.

Primacy

Related to anchoring is the issue of who goes first. Debaters, lawyers, politicians, and some negotiators always like to go first to capture the attention of those who are listening. Opening statements in debates and trials are like "first offers"—going first allows one to "claim" the argument space and frame the issues.

Availability

We are "primed" to see and consider what is most readily accessible to us—such as listed prices for houses, sticker prices for cars, ads we have seen or heard, what our friends tell us, and what we think the going rate, "norms," or customs are. Those who post high numbers are trying to use framing, anchoring, primacy, and availability to set expectations for negotiation responses. In many experiments, researchers suggested an irrelevant number (e.g. posting a very high number on a board or using a high number in a story) and then asked people how hot they think it is outside. Those exposed to the high (and irrelevant) number then say the temperature is actually much warmer than it is. Studies of real estate transactions have replicated these studies by exposing brokers to different (fictional) "appraisal" values and then finding that brokers/agents who have been exposed to higher numbers set higher prices, even if unrelated to actual values.

Vividness

As with primacy, we are all affected by what has just happened. Just after September 11, 2001, there was another fatal airline crash in New York. Almost everyone immediately assumed it was another terrorist attack. Subsequently, investigators found the cause to be pilot error. The vividness of a recent event causes us to create inaccurate assumptions of causation, motivation, or value. Skilled negotiators know how to use this device to "prime" listeners to react in ways they desire by choosing particularly vivid examples or anecdotes that will appeal to or frighten the other party into accepting value (and other) statements made by the speaker. Consider for how long after World War II Neville Chamberlain's "weakness" in negotiating with Hitler has become a vivid trope for urging other diplomats NOT to appear "weak." Vivid examples can be used either to encourage certain behaviors or to discourage them (appealing to human emotions such as fear, anger, love), demonstrating that these heuristics often operate simultaneously on both thinking and emotional processes.

Recency

Like vividness, but operating differently than primacy, some think it is more important to be the "last" to make an offer or an argument. This is why some negotiators (and lawyers and debaters) want to be the last to address the jury, judge, or audience so that offers and arguments can be reframed, rebutted, and recast, taking into account what has gone before.

All of these techniques are used to cast numbers and arguments in the light the user wishes. A sophisticated negotiator should know both how to use them but also how not to be taken in by them. Saying something first, vividly, or last should not necessarily frame the negotiation merits.

Endowment effects/prospect theory—status quo bias

In a widely replicated experiment, researchers have asked students to bargain over an item that half of the students are given by the researcher (a Business School mug, or a pen or water bottle) and half do not have. In thousands of iterations of this exercise the "sellers" of the item are unable to sell the item to the buyers. Having been "given" the item, it is now "owned" by the sellers and they value what they "have" more than those without the item. This is an example of "prospect theory" or the "endowment" or "status quo" bias. We value what we have more than those who do not have it. Sellers of houses, very attached to what they own, are thus more likely to set high prices not acceptable to would-be buyers. One of the conclusions is that we are biased toward what we have and it will cost us more to change the status quo. More recent work in this field has suggested that although this particular bias is very robust in many settings, it may be somewhat context dependent. (Who values pens in a time of computers? Who might really want a water bottle after running to class?)

Risk preferences—loss aversion, gains

Related to the phenomenon of status quo bias are the different values we place on negotiating for possible gains versus preventing or avoiding loss. Much of this research assumes that people should value "economic rationality," when often it might be "rational" to value other things, such as relationships or the possibility of repeat negotiations or other opportunities. In the examples below, consider what you would do and why.

Studies demonstrate that people will pay more to avoid a loss than to attempt to receive a gain. You have planned a night out with a friend. You have spent $100 on two concert tickets and made a reservation for dinner that will cost $100. In scenario # 1 you travel one hour to the restaurant to discover you have left your required paper tickets for the concert at home. Do you have your dinner and forgo the performance, or do you use the $100 in cash you have for dinner to buy new tickets at the venue? Now reverse, you get to the restaurant and discover you have the tickets and no cash (or credit card) with you to pay for the dinner. Do you sell your performance tickets to eat in the restaurant or forgo the dinner and just wait for the performance? In standard results of this exercise, most people go with what they have—eat in the restaurant and forget the performance if they have cash or skip the dinner and go to the performance if they have the tickets. This is the status quo/endowment effect—you value what is in your pocket. You do not want to add more costs (sunk costs) to "buy" something twice, the tickets in the first example, the dinner in the second. But, for years in my own classes the results have varied enormously depending on whether students value eating in a hard-to-get-a-reservation restaurant (foodies) more than a performance (they might stream later) or whether they value live performances more than overpriced meals. What we care about (values/preferences) really matters and not all human beings value things the same way. (Negotiation problem-solving test: can you figure out how to "negotiate" to get both the meal and the performance even if you don't have either the cash or the tickets?)

Now consider this problem. You receive a phone call from a lawyer who says an uncle you never knew has died and left you $100,000.

That's the good news. The bad news is that your cousins (his children), whom you don't know, are going to contest the will. The lawyer says you have an 80 percent chance of winning the case in court, in a trial that would happen in about two years (given court delays) and there would be $10,000 in legal fees and expenses. Your cousins have offered to settle by splitting the bequest now ($50,000 now). Do you take the offer of settlement or not? (80 percent chance of $100,000 = $80,000 minus legal fees, $10,000 = $70,000 in two years vs $50,000 now). Factors to consider (rationally) include expected and present economic value—is it really $50,000 vs $70,000 later? (How could $50,000 now be invested to yield more than $70,000 in two years?) What are your economic needs now (in debt or cash rich)? What will your needs be later? But there are also other social factors—do you want to adhere to your uncle's wishes? Do you want to challenge unknown relatives in court? Do you want to share with your cousins and meet your new relatives? Do you want to make a different offer or proposal? Do you trust the lawyer's assessment of the probable success rate? What you do in this negotiation will vary with your own risk preferences, your economic needs, and your attitudes toward relatives and family. My gambling risk-loving brother-in-law always chooses waiting for the trial, but most of my students choose taking the money now, as most have student debts. The unexpected money from the uncle is seen as a "windfall" to some, and social gain exists by not litigating and being nice to "new" cousins.

Think about this example—your boss offers you an opportunity to earn double wages for overtime work on a particular day that would give you an additional $1,000. But that evening is your anniversary and a planned dinner is very important to your partner. The person who values money would do the work; the person who values their relationship would turn down the offer to work overtime. The problem-solving negotiator could (1) ask their partner if they would prefer taking the extra money and moving the celebration to another night or (2) ask the boss if the overtime can be done another day or (3) what else can you think of?

Research studies on framing and aversion don't often replicate the conditions of the real world where there might be more room to alter the conditions and terms of the negotiation.

The lesson for negotiators in these examples is that how we "frame" offers, as potential gains or loss avoidance, can affect how negotiation offers are heard and whether they will be accepted. Most, but not all of us, would pay more to avoid a loss than to gamble on a potential gain. Another lesson here is to be careful not to let others "frame" or characterize what the negotiation is about, or what the value of particular proposals are to you. You can always reframe, make your own offers, and look for other items to trade, depending on your own goals and what *you* value.

With a focus on the examples above, look at whether you and your counterpart are framing in *words* (very likely to succeed, need very much) or in *numbers* (80 percent chance of success). People process preferences, offers, and risk analyses differently when they are expressed in numeric or narrative terms. Know how you (and your client if you are a lawyer or agent negotiator) are likely to listen to and process such information. Consider that whatever the aggregate statistics might be for a large population, whether or not something will happen to you (coin flip of heads), is actually more likely to be 50 percent (yes or no). Being assured the "cure" rate of a particular cancer treatment was 90 percent, my colleague, a statistician, pointed out to his doctor there were still 10 percent for whom the treatment did not work. In the simplest and most clichéd framing, optimists will see the glass as half full, while pessimists will see it as half empty. Neither is right or wrong; they simply reflect different perspectives which affect how information is presented and interpreted in negotiations.

Statistical errors

Almost everyone who is not a professional statistician makes "errors" when hearing or processing probability and risk information. A classic illustration of the kind of errors we all make is, like vividness, the law of small numbers. It is sometimes assumed that when a seemingly disproportionate group of people get cancer, there is a "cancer cluster" in a particular area. Often, however, what seems like a "lot" of people is not when the geographic area is expanded to include all those who are actually "exposed" to a particular risk. Related to this is the problem of "sample bias" when we make quantitative statements—"my regular customers are always happy with my work" (because those who are not happy with the work are no longer "regular" customers). When negotiators make claims about quality or statements about value of items, all good negotiators should ask to see (and separately evaluate) the data from which these claims are made.

Similarly, another common statistical error occurs when assessing causality—correlation is not causation. Consider: "There are more deaths from shark bites when more ice cream cones are sold." Does the eating of ice cream cones "cause" people to be "tastier" to the sharks? Or is there "an intervening cause" or correlated event—both shark bites and ice cream sales occur in the summer when people are swimming in the ocean. So, when a negotiator asserts value because of some causative factor, consider what else might be "causing" values to climb or fall.

Would you rather have a 50 percent share of a business worth $100,000 or 20 percent of a business worth $500,000? When people offer percentages (especially when mentioned first) we often look at the percentages, rather than the principal amount—especially risky when we are evaluating numbers that can change (the value of a company in sales, projected profits, risks of harm from pollutants, etc.). Some crafty negotiators will use seemingly very precise numbers ("the offer is $143,987.00 based on our assessment of value"), to justify what is, in fact, arbitrarily set. Bargaining over numbers tends to result in reflexive reactions, including arbitrary concessions and "split the difference" compromises, especially when we don't take time to "do the math." Consider if a bat and a ball cost $1.10 together and the bat costs $1.00 more than the ball, how much does the ball cost? (Did you say 10c? Wrong! The ball costs 5c and the bat costs $1.05.) What do the numbers stand for (in value)? How accurate are they? A good negotiator should ask—"how did you arrive at that value? Let's explore the math together." Slow the conversation until you are sure there is agreement of the predictions and claimed worth being asserted. If needed, seek expert help from an accountant, statistician, or mathematician, or someone with experience in the industry.

Social issues, errors, and biases: Labeling

A close relative of the power of framing and anchoring is the sociological concept of labeling or categorizing. Whoever puts a name on something with words or a value with numbers with greater numeracy skill is attempting to control the terms of the negotiation. Classic studies have shown that when children are "labeled" as either "gifted" or "slow," regardless of the accuracy of the classification, their teachers then treat them as super-intelligent or incapable of learning and then we observe a "self-fulfilling prophecy" in the result. Those treated as "smart" will get extra attention and harder tasks to complete and will seem smarter when later examined.

Most of advertising and attempts to persuade in negotiation use those grandiose adjectives to tell you that you are about to bid on "the best," the "premium," "the Rolls Royce of…" to control associations of value in your thinking. Consider how we approach the labels of "plaintiff vs defendant," "labor or management," and even "buyer and seller." In a famous exercise in a Stanford University social psychology class, students were asked to play the same Prisoner's Dilemma game. The group that was told they were playing "the Social Work" game were more likely to "cooperate" with each other (maximizing group scores) than those who were told they were playing "the Wall Street" game (who played to maximize individual scores by defecting against others in the game).

Reactive devaluation

A special case of the distortions of labeling effects is called reactive devaluation. Reactive devaluation occurs when we devalue or can't hear what "the other side" has said because of who they are in relation to us. Plaintiffs think an offer to settle a lawsuit from a defendant is always too low, the defendant thinks the offer from the plaintiff is far too high. Republicans devalue any plan for taxation and spending when made by a Democrat and Democrats devalue what Republicans propose. Some of this is, of course, based on political principles, ideologies, and differences in values, but often there is simple arbitrary rejection of what one's opponent suggests, even if there might be some merit in the proposal.

In testing this theory, psychologist Lee Ross set up an experiment when college campuses were actively seeking disinvestment in companies operating in apartheid South Africa. Students on many campuses demanded immediate disinvestment; boards of directors of universities were unwilling (primarily for financial reasons); faculty and some university administrators proposed more gradual disinvestment. Ross put forward three variations on these proposals with labels "Student Proposal," "Board of Directors Proposal," and "Faculty Proposal" (varying the content in all three treatments to be versions of the three different proposals). Regardless of the content of the proposal, the students always voted for the Student Proposal and against the Board of Directors proposal. The "label" trumped all consideration of the actual merits of the proposal. Good negotiators need to think about the labeling used in their proposals and might want to engage a mediator to "neutralize" the presentation of offers and proposals with content that is assessed on its own merits—not the assumed attributes of the proposers.

Attribution

The psychological processes which lead us to "devalue" what others say because of who they are is part of a larger process of how we assign blame and responsibility. Research studies have found that whether we attribute credit or blame to ourselves, to others, or to "forces beyond our control" is often structured by who we already are. Stereotypes and assumed characteristics also play a large role in attribution of causation, credit, and blame. Women are more likely to attribute good events or achievements to "luck" and bad events or outcomes to themselves. Men tend to do the reverse: success or achievements are their own and bad things happen to them because of luck or factors beyond their control. Women often assume or take on blame (as do those of ethnic or racial minorities) and attribute success to luck or others (mentors, friends, and family), and men (and whites) assume they are deserving of all they achieve and fail only when someone or something else is to blame. This has enormous impact on what people ask for and accept (concessions, compromises) in many kinds of negotiations (e.g. salary negotiations).

Overconfidence

American radio host and writer Garrison Keillor, in his long-lasting program *Lake Wobegon*, spoke of the place where "all the children are above average." Many negotiations fail because both sides are overly optimistic about what they can achieve, the value of what they are "selling" or negotiating (e.g. the merits of a legal case for lawyers, the value of a house or a company in sales). In several studies of legal negotiations, Randall Kiser found that both plaintiff and defense counsel were shown to overvalue their cases and therefore failed to reach settlement agreements when they should have. In the American legal system, lawyers who refuse settlement offers and then do "worse" when they go to trial must pay the legal fees of the side that offered the settlement which was rejected. Data from several US states demonstrated that plaintiffs were wrong in refusing offers more often (as a matter of frequency) but defendants, though "wrong" in refusing settlement offers less often, were more likely to be really wrong when they refused a settlement offer because their losses were of greater magnitude. Lawyers who had served as mediators (in other matters) were less likely to make overly confident claims and were more likely to settle and avoid losses, perhaps conditioned by their third-party experience of evaluation of other cases to moderate their own demands.

Confirmation

Similarly, many people tend, in the questions they ask or the information they seek, to look for confirmation of what they already believe to be true, rather than seeking disconfirming information, which could usefully adjust claims of value to more accurate levels.

Contrast effects

Another distortion in our thinking when we negotiate is the "contrast" effect. We react or respond in an automatic way to a contrast of what has been offered and such concepts as "relative deprivation" or "I want what she is having" cause us to value something just because someone else has it—the "have nots" want what the "haves" have. Or consider, some friends are out for dinner and half want white wine and half want red wine—with an inability to choose, one suggests that a "contrast" compromise (rosé) is a good solution. But is it? None of the diners want rosé so it is a bad choice. Better solution? How about a half bottle of red and a half bottle of white? Contrasts often limit us to reactions or "opposites" and may inhibit more creative solutions which are not simply reactive.

Hindsight bias

Yet another impediment to good thinking in negotiation is hindsight bias. When the negotiation is over, we assume that what we did led to the outcomes we achieved, assuming causality—"we knew it all along" or "see, what we did was right," which, rightly or wrongly, over-attributes our own actions and tends to under-attribute both what the other parties do or what may have happened due to external factors. For many this is overconfidence or belief in one's own efficacy. Some of these biases are actually more complex: some are gendered and socially constituted—women are less likely to take credit for effectiveness, but to assume self-blame, as are other less "dominant" groups, such as minorities and neophytes. One of the dangers of hindsight bias is that we may "overlearn," by thinking that if we believe something "went well" before, we should do it again, without considering if the situation is different in a subsequent interaction.

Social issues—demographics, implicit and explicit biases

One important context of negotiation is who the parties are and how they see each other. Most of us are aware of explicit biases we might have—racism, sexism, classism, ageism (cutting both ways against younger or older negotiators), religious bias (evidenced by reactions to veils, turbans, crosses, and skullcaps in our multicultural world). Although acting in a discriminatory way in a negotiation might be prohibited in many legal systems (in employment, public-governmental settings, some contracting, housing) most negotiations are conducted in private spaces not visible to others. So even explicit bias still plays a distorting role in many negotiations—with assumptions and stereotypes as impediments to working on the substantive issues.

These biases are described as pertaining to individuals negotiating with each other, but consider how they operate at group, organizational, and national levels too. The "smaller" non-aligned nations created their own alternative groups (to the Security Council) to challenge power-based assumptions at the United Nations. Trade unions and other collective groups were formed historically to thwart the more powerful employers in labor negotiations and to counter assumptions of "weakness." Many civil rights, human rights, gay rights, and women's rights movements use aggregation to claim power in negotiations from those biased against them.

In recent decades, sociologists and psychologists have also demonstrated that all of us have "implicit" biases—meaning we may not even be aware of the fact that we are using stereotypes in how we respond to each other. Men make assumptions about women (more emotional, "easy" push-overs); women about men (bullying "mansplainers"); whites make assumptions about blacks (less experienced, less educated), blacks about whites (entitled, privileged, biased); young people have little experience, older people can't process information or use technology. We construct our behaviors quickly (System I automatic thinking) by looking at skin color, nationality, religious clothing, assumed gender or sexual orientation, age, even size, to say things or do things in negotiation that may turn out to be not only morally wrong but instrumentally ill advised.

Implicit bias operates on both sides of a negotiation. The objects of stereotypical thinking (which can include "positive" associations such as Asians are better at maths) are often likely to have internalized assumptions about their "group" in their own behaviors, called "stereotype threat." Women and blacks may be less confident with white males, women may assume "too much" cooperation will come when negotiating with other women. Combining bias with attribution and labeling theory, social psychologists have been able to demonstrate that "priming" or changing the label of a person (or group) before a negotiation can indeed affect behavior ("de-biasing" by coaching). If your boss, mother, teacher, or partner says "you can do this" you may raise your own expectations about your performance. But be careful not to "overcompensate"—hopefully our mothers and partners love us so they might be biased themselves (this is affinity bias—yet another one to look out for). Get some feedback from an outsider.

Bias blind spots

Yet another bias, combining implicit bias and overconfidence, is a blind spot bias to our own biases. Most of us think, "I would never be a racist, sexist, classist—I treat everyone fairly. That bias and discrimination stuff—that is what other people do." Cognitive research has demonstrated how powerfully this operates in human behavior. Our ability to correct for these biases is limited. Modern cognitive research is engaged in looking at what can work in interrupting very old and common patterns of interaction. However, so far all those "de-biasing" training sessions employed in so many workplaces have not demonstrated great success. Once taken out of the training site (laboratory, workplace, school) people reflexively revert to what is so deeply programmed within them. Some of this may be generational and may change over time as our societies become more multicultural and people interact with people different from themselves.

Moods, emotions, physical environment, and food influences on negotiation

How we "feel" greatly affects how we perform in negotiation. It is now well documented that those who are in a bad mood, have just received some bad news, are tired, hungry, uncomfortable, or angry will not do well in negotiation. Such mood states prevent the processing of information, inhibit creativity, and are likely to lead to "irrational" escalation. This is one condition over which we can have some control—eat some chocolate, get a good night's sleep, meditate, dress comfortably, take a bathroom break, as well as prepare and remain calm at all times, but certainly pay attention to emotional and physical states in negotiation. They are there and affecting everything we do. Warren Christopher, former Secretary of State of the United States, said his success in negotiation was that, unlike others, he did not need to sleep, eat, or go to the bathroom (persistence, patience, and presence were his behavioral attributes, with little acknowledgment of moods or emotional needs).

Emotional attachments can also have other effects on our negotiation behaviors. Research demonstrates that when a relationship is more important than the substance of the negotiation we negotiate differently—we "give more" to friends, family, and repeat players (trying to keep a reliable supplier happy). This may be exactly what we want to do with those we love or with whom we interact frequently, but we also need to be attentive to when we might have done better by taking more time to consider options, rather than just compromising or being reflexively generous.

Winner's curse/buyer's remorse

The saddest error of all is when we have successfully concluded a negotiation and then ask, did I agree too quickly/for too much/too little? Did I agree without having enough information? Knowing what the other side valued? Anyone who completes a negotiation with *low intensity of offers* (just one or two rounds) knows this feeling—what did I do wrong? So, we want to do well in a negotiation but in our culture of negotiation haggling and the "dance of negotiation" we must feel like we have "earned" the result we achieve—should we have negotiated harder, longer, gotten more information, had some expert advice? This regret factor keeps negotiators up at night. We can learn from the "winner's curse" each time. Just before we reach final agreement— how are we going to feel about this tomorrow? Stop, consider, and ask for an outside opinion.

What should we do to correct our errors and biases? Is de-biasing possible?

Is it possible to keep all these distortions in our thinking and behaving in our mind as we plan and conduct negotiations? The answer is probably not. There is a limit to what one mind can process at one time, especially when engaged in interactive communication with others. Yet one important corrective to virtually all of these is, when you can, *Slow down* and do as much "deliberative" thinking (System II) both before and during a negotiation as you can. What assumptions am I making about (1) the other parties? (2) what is at stake? (3) what I (or my client) want? and (4) what it is possible to achieve here? Structure and plan for negotiations to minimize defaults to automatic thinking. Schedule for more than one meeting; don't be pressured to negotiate with tight deadlines, use time during breaks in the negotiation for more research, feedback from others, and development of new options.

Next, remember the key behavior for good problem-solving negotiation is *ask questions* (before making statements or demands). *Getting more information* (through research, working with experts or others outside a negotiation, and from the other side itself) can help correct for the assumptions we have. Determine what the other side really values, avoiding the assumptions of scarcity or false equivalence of value for all parties. Always *ask for rationales, principles, and justifications of proposals from the other parties, exposing arithmetic calculations, sources of data, predictions, assumed causality, and test what is said.* For a graphic example of this, consider how the use of serious statistics (batting averages, pitches, runs, fielding) in baseball player negotiations in *Moneyball* exposed false assumptions of player talent as teams negotiated for particular players based solely on coaches' or scouts' "biased" observations and claims.

You should always *be aware of classic negotiation ploys* (high first demands, exaggerations of value, inaccurate statistical or numerical values, irrational escalation) and *prepare for responses* ("moves and turns") including *more questions, "landmine tests," deflection, confrontation, reframing or taking a break, or, if necessary, walking away* (or training yourself not to *overreact* to what others do). Other useful approaches here are to be careful about *setting the agenda, scripting and planning in advance what you will have to say to counter what others may do, consider all the possible behaviors (and proposals and offers) in advance, consider changing the negotiators at the table* (going up the supervisory chain in an organization, getting an agent or lawyer, or even replacing yourself if necessary).

Engaging in creative problem solving also allows for developing such good options that the possible substantive outcome of the negotiation may move through the interpersonal, psychological, or social impediments, described in this chapter, to reaching a good agreement. What *parts* of a negotiation can be dealt with first (disaggregation, incremental or contingent agreements)? Should general goals and principles be agreed to first to assure references to *benchmarks* and *common principles* as the negotiation proceeds? Keeping attention on the actual goals of a negotiation can help focus on the ends, not only the means, of negotiation.

Finally, it is sometimes useful to "debias" a negotiation by getting some help from a third party—a *mediator*. Mediators who have been trained with attention to all of the cognitive, social, psychological, emotional, cultural, and behavioral biases can help the parties see what is blocking their possible agreement because they have experience as outsiders to many kinds of negotiations. Mediators can be negotiators' negotiators. Having substantive and process expertise, they can help those in trouble or impasse overcome some of the challenges outlined here.

Chapter 6
Complex multi-party multi-issue negotiations

How do multi-party, multi-issue negotiations differ from two-party negotiations? There are issues of what constitutes agreement-consent, coalition formation, sequencing and commitments, decision rules, vetoes and holdouts, side agreements, process rules, consensus building, dispute system design, and cultural issues. Different approaches to complex negotiations, including the use of third-party assistants, may be necessary when there are more than two parties.

The most difficult issues in negotiation theory and practice are the problems of complexity and numbers. What happens to all the basic concepts of agreement, ZOPA, Alternatives to Negotiation, offers, concessions, commitments, proposals, and frameworks of negotiation when there are more than two parties negotiating? Much modern conflict resolution and negotiation theory was developed during the Cold War to study the conflicts between two axes of power, which inspired modern game theory and its focus on competition and coordination. It is probably no coincidence that the Nobel prize-winning game theory (awarded to John Nash and Thomas Schelling, among others), which initially focused on two-party strategic actions, was so evocative in developing negotiation theory with its assumptions of scarce resources. For example, money, land, water, and other resources were assumed to be divisible by two parties in conflict, which led to the behavioral prescriptions about how to "distribute" such scarce resources competitively.

More recently, both scholars and practitioners have recognized that few disputes or transactions have only two parties. Virtually all legal matters involve more than two parties whether legally liable, or financially or socially affected by any resolution. Also involved are insurers, employees, suppliers, vendors, family members, partners in business or personal lives, so that almost no lawsuits are only two-party conflicts. All diplomatic negotiations and all transactional negotiations resulting in contracts, new entities, or organizations also affect many parties, even those not at the negotiation.

Numbers in negotiation: From one to many

How do the numbers of participants in a negotiation affect both how we conceptualize the negotiation issues (the "science" of negotiation) and how we should behave (the "art" of negotiation)? Consider the different issues that arise with different numbers of participants:

Number	Issues of process or outcome
N = 1	Internal negotiation with self
N = 2	"Classic" negotiation choices—distributive, integrative
	Compete or collaborate, outcome is two-party agreement
N = 3	Coalition, alliance formation, what is agreement?
	Consent of all or some?
	Commitments, blocking, vetoes
N = 4	Two-party negotiations with agents, lawyers, or four-way negotiation, what is decision rule for agreement?
N = 3 or 5	Negotiators, with or without agents and a third party
	Mediator/facilitator, decision rules, information-sharing issues
N > 5	Need for formal agenda, information sharing, decision rules, need for facilitator
N > 25	Organizations, groups, communities—process rules, agenda, leader-facilitator, formal or informal, voting rules
N > 100	Large groups, political entities, agenda, information, process rules, decision rules, public or private, representativeness, agency issues
N > 200	International treaty negotiations, large group deliberation, meeting management, leadership, process and decision rules (voting methods), plenary or caucus (committee); transparency of deliberations, records
N > beyond 200	Polity, governments, very large organizations, agents and representatives, speaking and deliberation rules, open or closed processes, decision rules, facilitators, leaders, voting, consent, legitimacy, transparency or private deals, coalitions.

What is a negotiated agreement with more than two parties? Measures of consent, Zones of Possible Agreement

In a classic two-party negotiation it is easy to know if there is an agreement—both parties must consent. When a third party is added to a negotiation whether there is an agreement becomes more problematic. Is it enough if two agree and cut out the third? What if two think they have agreed and then the excluded third party offers a better deal and upends the prior deal? The question of whether there is an agreement is itself a negotiable issue. Any negotiation involving more than two people needs a "*decision rule*." What will constitute an agreement, especially if the parties want to ensure some protection against defections. In complex international treaty negotiations there is almost always a provision for how many signatories are necessary for the treaty to come into force.

Adding a third party to a negotiation can easily complicate any ZOPA as there may be different preferences among the three parties on any or all issues. A decision rule can require all parties to agree to any final agreement that is reached (a *unanimous* rule) that would encompass all the issues, or it is possible for different agreements to be reached on different issues (some with two in agreement and others with all three). Imagine, as happens in legislative negotiations, a process of *log rolling*—one party agrees to vote on a law for a colleague (such as an appropriation to build a special project in his district) but only if a third party agrees to vote on approving one of his projects. This can be a three-way trade, common to many kinds of agreements, especially with conditions for bank loans, guarantors, insurance, and many kinds of international treaties.

Consider how the "promise" of international aid or military assistance (or the "threat" to remove it) affects how the recipient of such aid may behave in military or diplomatic situations. In the

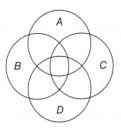

5. **Venn diagram: interlocking parties and issues.**

International Whaling Convention, which seeks to ban and regulate whaling capture, votes (affecting Japan, Norway, Russia, and other countries) have been affected by side payments of aid to non-whaling countries who are members of the Whaling Commission. This example also illustrates the concept of *linkage* in determining what a possible ZOPA can be. Some of the two-way or side negotiations may be about issues that are separate from the primary terms being negotiated.

Multi-party negotiations invariably also involve multiple issues. Deciding which are relevant to a particular deal may change or vary in importance among the parties. All the terms of a potential agreement may be dependent on what each party can get from one of the others. It might be nearly impossible here to map in two- (think three-) dimensional space all the possible terms that could meet the different needs of each party. Think how changing outcomes to make one party better off without harming one or more others becomes complicated when there are multiple parties. Without clear decision rules about when an agreement is reached, virtually any agreement will be unstable unless all parties agree because there is always the possibility of another deal being made with another party. There might be ZOPAs with some, but not all, of the parties and there might be overlapping ZOPAs on some issues, but not all. Imagine a Venn diagram with many circles of parties and issues with some overlapping and some not (Figure 5).

Alternatives to negotiated agreements? How many?

When any party to a multi-party negotiation considers whether to agree to something they must consider what other agreements are possible. Are there better ones with these parties? With other parties not yet at the table? What bad things (WATNAs) can happen if I don't stay in this particular negotiation with these people? Should I look for other parties with whom to negotiate? Although it is not impossible to map a range of other possible negotiations, multi-party, multi-issue negotiations are harder to cabin in advance as so many moving pieces may change, as more people make proposals either to all the parties together or to some separately.

Information sharing and processing

When there are more than two parties (and especially as sub-groups and alliances are formed in large group negotiations) the provision and processing of information also becomes more difficult. Will all parties share information equally with all others? Should there be mutually agreed disclosure rules? If one party receives "confidential" information from another (within a coalition or as an attempt to change loyalties) should that information be disclosed to others? In large formal negotiations there might be negotiated rules that require transparency but in all negotiations, formal or otherwise, there is little one can do to totally control the use of information. The seasoned negotiator in these complex settings needs to be vigilant about analyzing what information is to be revealed to whom and how to assess and test information provided by others. In litigation there is formal information exchange (discovery in US practice), but there is also always the use of more hidden sources of information (consider spies, private detectives, defectors, former associates of negotiating parties, whistleblowers, disgruntled customers, spouses, competitors, and others).

Coalitions, alliances, commitments, defections, and holdouts

Any group of three children playing together can demonstrate how unstable a playgroup is. When I was a child it was common for some of the "mean girls" with whom I grew up to start with three and then leave one girl "flat" by excluding her. The "left out" girl would then do whatever she could to offer (bribe) one of the other girls to come play with her (candy, dolls). That would last until the newly excluded girl would destabilize the agreement with other enticements. This sad tale of young girl play (competition, not collaboration) has often been enacted in international diplomacy and alliance formation. Consider the tragedy of World War I where "the enemy of my enemy is my friend" politics linked two alliances of the Austro-Hungarian and Ottoman empires with Germany against France, Great Britain, and Russia (with their own prior conflicts), ending with its own disastrous negotiation, the Treaty of Versailles. This in turn planted the seeds of a new war (World War II) also with temporary alliances (US, France, Great Britain, and the Soviet Union), which in turn transformed into new alliances in the Cold War West (NATO) vs Soviet Bloc (Warsaw Pact). Consider also how that Warsaw Pact in turn crumbled when, after challenges to the internal reforms in the Soviet Union, one country after another defected from the pact by declaring independence from both the Soviet Union and then the Warsaw Pact itself.

In any alliance or coalition there is the problem of commitments (signed, collateralized, pledges, or writing) and defections (simple exits or moves to other alliances or deals). Once the numbers of negotiators increases from two, almost any agreement can be unstable without clear undertakings and enforcement provisions. Of course, two-party negotiated agreements are sometimes breached, but more than two-party negotiations tend to be more unstable and may require additional terms of incentives or penalties.

Related to the problem of *defection* is the issue of *vetoes* or *holdouts* if there are agreements about how a coalition will decide its moves. If groups of negotiators form sub-groups and there are customs or procedures for agreement for both process and substantive outcome, any single member may sabotage or prevent agreement by holding out for what it wants or vetoing what the rest of the group wants. In practical terms this is an *internal negotiation* within the group and may turn on who has *power* within any alliance. Consider how President George W. Bush constituted a "coalition of the willing" in the wars in Afghanistan and Iraq in the early 2000s (by using both carrots and sticks of granting or withholding American aid). Groups that negotiate within themselves and then with other groups will want to consider how decisions are made about both process and substantive matters. In any negotiation where one of the parties is a group (e.g. trade union, organizational departments, factions within a dispute, or different allegiances within a political party, country, or other grouping), getting and keeping the parties sufficiently aligned to negotiate with "other" parties is itself a complex multi-party negotiation of coordination.

Process and ground rules

When there are many parties and multiple issues in a negotiation it is often useful for an official agenda and a set of ground rules for deliberation to be separately negotiated. In the negotiation of the Northern Ireland Easter Peace Accords more than a year was spent developing rules of engagement including decommissioning of arms, speaking and talking rules, permitted participants (prohibiting violent individuals), representation rules, and some rules about separate meetings (caucuses) and sanctions for process rule violations. In the three-month deliberations which formed the United States constitution in 1787 two full days were spent on process rules. These rules included: confidentiality of the deliberations, attendance rules (voting only when all were present in the plenary sessions) and speaking rules (only two comments per delegate per issue and no speaking a second time until all who wanted to address the issue had done so). In addition, the delegates developed task groups to work on specific issues (rather than full plenary deliberations on each issue), assigning roles of a recorder (James Madison), a "neutral" leader of the meeting (George Washington, who spoke only once on a matter of substance), and a process commentator (Benjamin Franklin, who often appealed to prayer to calm heated negotiations). The delegates also used voting rules that included no attribution to particular individuals (now known as *Chatham House* rules), votes to allow reconsideration of previously agreed-to items in order to encourage *linkage*, *trades*, *contingent agreements*, and *compromise*, and, finally, an agreement that the final document would be voted on *in toto* (preparing the way for seeking the legitimacy of the finished agreement for a contested ratification process). As is common in so many large number negotiations, it was assumed that a majority vote of states (12 in attendance out of 13) and delegates (55 present) would control decision making.

In modern complex negotiations it is often useful to have *process experts* (facilitators, mediators, and consensus builders) to help frame and manage the process of difficult negotiations seeking to accomplish a particular outcome, such as in urban planning, environmental regulations, community relations, budget allocations, legislation, and international treaties. Professional process experts can help groups negotiate their own ground rules in an effort to help legitimacy and enforcement of those self-imposed ground rules. They may use a template of ground rules which have been used with other groups (e.g. no interruptions, use of a "talking stick" to rotate turns of speaking, contingency or revision rules, and prohibitions on violence, insults, threats, or other counter-productive actions in the deliberations).

Decision rules and voting

When negotiating with multiple parties, how do we know an agreement has been reached? In complex settings it is useful to agree on *decision rules for the substantive terms* of any agreement. This is a complicated issue and is affected by mathematics, game theory, and strategic voting theory. How we vote has enormous consequences for what agreements can be reached. Negotiators should understand the implications of each possible method of voting.

In Western democracies the default voting rules for most decisions is *majority* rule (50 percent + 1 of all voters). This assumes all votes count equally, but sometimes they do not. The European Union, the World Bank, and other organizations allocate percentage of voting powers by financial contributions, size of population, GNP, or some other "weighted" expression of power so that some members have a greater "share" of votes. The majority voting rule is often efficient for reaching a decision which has some strong support (but not total consensus), but it also means that a very large minority (49.99 percent) might be unhappy with the final decisions. All voting rules are also subject to "rules within the rules" that affect outcomes. Is it a majority of votes cast (including abstentions)? Of those eligible to vote? Those present at the meeting? Some groups and organizations use more demanding voting rules for greater legitimacy of the decision—some form of *super-majority* voting rule such as a 2/3 or 3/4 or even total *unanimity* of those voting. Where a single entity can veto the will of the majority (such as in the United Nations Security Council) even a super-majority rule will not authorize an agreement.

Consider the different effects of different voting rules. Simple majority of votes cast is easier to obtain but also potentially unstable with a strong dissenting minority. Super-majority votes may be harder to obtain (taking more time to bring more people along) but once achieved may have greater acceptance. Seeking total *consensus* or close to it can motivate the parties to seek more creative solutions to meet more of the needs and preferences of all parties. Or, more problematically, searching for unanimous agreement or total consensus can lead to "satisficing" (not optimal) compromises or the "lowest common denominator."

An example can illustrate what difference voting rules make. Hiring appointments to university faculties can use any of these rules. A majority vote means most, but not all, agree on a candidate. But not requiring everyone to agree may yield greater diversity of successful candidates. For many years at least one university department required unanimity—total consensus for appointment, assuming that was a high standard for the quality of the candidate. But it resulted in a faculty with similar views about controversial issues in the field, and not much diversity. The 2/3 and 3/4 rules provide a middle point, where most, but not all, agree on an appointment so some dissent is permitted, but a greater degree of acceptability to "most" is also assured. These voting rules and their consequences are especially important when groups vote on many things, so that there may be *linkages* or a *history of voting patterns* that affect each vote. Another form of voting issue here is log rolling or trading of votes to affect particular outcomes—if you vote for my candidate now, I will vote for yours next time.

Voting on preferences for a negotiation (especially when deciding among and between possible options) is complicated by a variety of mathematical paradoxes. The *Condorcet paradox* tells us that how people will vote may turn on the order in which options are presented. Consider that there are three parties and three options from which to choose. When preferences differ among the parties' rankings 1, 2, and 3, the parties may decide to vote on each sequentially. When this is done, option A defeats B, and B ranked against C might be first, but what happens when C defeats A? In sequential voting those options that come later will tend to do better than those that come first (seeming to be a better comparison). Compare this to anchor effects with a single proposal or offer. Clever negotiators in multi-party and multi-issue settings will know how to manipulate presentations of proposals to effect the result they desire. When individuals vote in group settings, with different preferences ranked when there are multiple issue options, it might be impossible (the *impossibility theorem*) to ever determine a single *stable preference of the whole group for all the issues*. In these settings votes may be taken on single issues to determine preferences but when multiple issues are combined to create a "package" proposal, preferences may differ and aggregation of different issues will provide what is called an *intransitive* (unstable) preference. This may be exacerbated when new proposals (linked or seriatim) are presented by the other parties to the negotiation and parties have different preferences with respect to different elements of the proposal.

A serious problem in any voting situation is *strategic voting*, which is the misrepresentation of true preferences in order to block other proposals or to manipulate voting rules. Returning to the example of faculty voting, if we have a limited number of jobs to offer and we need a ranking of candidates for a preference vote, people can put last those candidates whom they think others will favor in order to move them to the bottom of aggregate voting.

Some voting problems have no simple or mathematical solutions but they can be managed by having the parties fully understand how voting rules may actually affect the substance of what they are deciding. Professional facilitators can help manage such processes by explaining both process rules and decision rules before any substantive negotiations occur. In the international negotiations for what became the Kyoto Environmental Clean Air Accords, professionals were engaged to provide instructions to the diplomatic negotiators present so that power imbalances in negotiation expertise might be reduced. Part of such pre-negotiation training can also help advise parties that are representatives of larger groups to develop protocols for assessing client preferences and communication rules for sharing (media relations) or keeping confidential interim proposals. Remember that although transparency often sounds like a good value, making public commitments can hinder more creative solutions and constrict what negotiators may be authorized to do.

Sequencing issues and parties

When we know negotiations will involve more than one party, we have to decide whether to form an alliance in advance. Should I negotiate first with my friends and get them on board or should I try to start with the tougher people to win over? Is the enemy of my enemy my friend? In a description of these negotiation dilemmas in international relations, James Sebenius described how context matters in making such choices of *sequencing* the order in which parties might be approached. He noted that the two American presidents, George H. W. Bush and George W. Bush (using some of the same advisors), made different sequencing choices for successful formation of coalitions. When Iraq invaded Kuwait in 1990, the senior Bush wanted to take military action after securing congressional approval. He knew that the American legislators and public were still deeply affected by the massive losses of lives and reputation in the Vietnam war and feared that congressional approval would not be forthcoming. So, Bush (Senior), working with experienced diplomats, sought to create a coalition of Arab states (and persuaded Israel not to take separate action if attacked) to go to the UN for an international resolution. Only after successfully obtaining a UN Security Council Resolution (using the international community first) did George Bush (Senior) go to the US Congress for approval of military action. In contrast, following the September 11, 2001 attacks on the New York World Trade Center, George W. Bush, with widespread and unparalleled unity of the American people, went immediately to the US Congress for approval to attack Afghanistan, and then later announced that a "coalition of the willing" (assembled with use of carrots and sticks in foreign aid) would join the effort. George Bush Senior did not go to his "own people" (Congress) first, but only after amassing an international coalition did he ask for authorization from his own nation. George Bush Junior needed quick approval and was able to go to his "own people" and capitalize on the outrage after the attack on the US to blunt the possible disapproval of the larger international community.

These vivid examples illustrate the importance of sequencing, or what Sebenius calls "backward mapping," in multi-party coalitional settings: thinking what outcome we might desire in a negotiation with multiple parties—to whom do I need to talk and in what order? What deference patterns are there? Which party do I need to bring the others along? As political strategist and former mayor of Chicago Bill Daley once said, "can we find the guy who can deliver the guy?" Working backward from desired results we plan avenues for getting the right people lined up to join us in our appeals to get others to join us and form final deals.

How one approaches other parties is itself an issue of negotiation—does one work in secret, making the same promises or side deals to multiple parties (and risking a reputation of being seen as a duplicitous and secretive operator) or does one make public offerings (bids and auctions) to see who is willing to offer something to be a part of a coalition? In major multi-party negotiations, like international diplomatic negotiations, it is useful to consider whether there should be prohibitions or limitations on the number or location of private (caucus) meetings (to the extent such rules can be enforced). In many multi-party negotiations, one cannot truly regulate how parties will meet with each other (in private conversations, over meals, etc.). The war in Vietnam ended with "back table" ("dual track") negotiations in Paris, as did the US–Iran hostage negotiations in 1980. Some think that Benjamin Franklin's tavern-pub diplomacy in Philadelphia, charming and cajoling the delegates to the US constitutional convention, did as much to bring unfriendly bedfellows together as the more formal constitutional drafting meetings.

Groupthink and dissent

While many focus on the difficulty of reaching consensus in any group setting, research in sociology, psychology, and organizational behavior suggests that deliberating groups can also have the opposite problem: *groupthink*, hindering the consideration of ideas coming from outside of that group. When like-minded people are in a group they may reinforce their preconceived notions and fail to see other important considerations. Consider the current political gridlock in many countries—Democratic–Republican in the US; Labour and Tory, Remain and Leave in Brexit—in which views on particular issues are "locked in" based on assumed shared beliefs of group members. Extreme *polarization* (a variant on the problem of reactive devaluation considered in the previous chapter) means those inside a group have their views confirmed by those like themselves, discounting anything coming from the "other side," consequently blocking consideration of ideas or options outside of the familiar norms. For these reasons, many point to the importance of *dissent* and brainstorming in any group to encourage consideration of more options and to expand the range of proposals.

Facilitation/mediation/consensus building

These issues and others, including power imbalances, representativeness, and accountability of agents or spokespeople for groups in negotiation, suggest that complex multi-party negotiation may benefit from more formal structures, with facilitators and consensus-building professionals. These professionals are knowledgeable in managing meetings, agenda development, process rules and design, voting and other decision-making choices, and can assist negotiators in varying contexts to deal with issues of interest and needs specification, emotional, political, and other differences to create the process which is appropriate for the situation. Good negotiators, trying to achieve agreements in many different spheres, must learn to work with *process pluralism* or *appropriate dispute resolution* (ADR).

Facilitators are process managers, expected to be neutral and unconnected to the parties, and can help design and enforce ground rules, process rules, voting, and decision rules.

Mediators are facilitators of negotiation, third-party "neutrals" who may sometimes be known to the parties or chosen for their substantive expertise. They manage negotiation processes, but also help the parties by facilitating creative solutions. They often coach parties (in caucus or joint sessions) on communication issues. They may also assist in evaluating proposals (called "reality testing") and suggest ideas themselves. In international relations, some mediators are known as "muscle mediators" by making promises to the parties to provide aid or other incentives if the parties themselves come to an agreement. Mediators do not decide anything substantive—that would be a different process of arbitration or adjudication. But mediators can be especially effective at asking questions and encouraging parties to explore their doubts, curiosity about the other party, or need for more information, and they can encourage a more empathic interpersonal process to enhance communication and mutual understanding.

Consensus builders are a newer form of professional negotiation assistance. These negotiation experts do case analyses, stakeholder review, agenda drafting, and problem mapping (through detailed interviews of interested parties and interest groups) to facilitate more formal negotiations in public policy, community, regulatory, and international settings and, increasingly, in crisis or highly conflictual situations as in social protests.

Modes of complex negotiation

Complex negotiations involve many different kinds of issues, including constitutive (constitutional, organization formation, partnerships), more temporary or ad hoc agreements, or single issue, task-based negotiation with many parties. Some negotiations are intended to result in primarily permanent agreements (ante-nuptial agreements, constitutions, treaties, corporate Articles of Incorporation) and others are more contingent and will be revisable (by-laws, employment contracts), while other negotiations may be one-off engagements. Some negotiations will involve claims about values in arguments; other negotiations may involve strong emotions or political commitments. Some negotiations may involve more than one kind of discourse (reason, passion, morals, politics) requiring the "middle" path of bargaining and negotiation to provide options for reconciling differing interests. Table 3 illustrates some different kinds of negotiations which might be assisted by different models of direct party or facilitated negotiation.

Political scientist Jon Elster illustrated the effects of different negotiation processes by contrasting the formative processes of the United States and French constitutions, accomplished in the same historical period (1787–91). The French, using what philosophers would call "first principles," opted for open, largely public and plenary deliberations, which were announced to the public daily in the equivalent of the modern press conference. The Americans developed a task-based division of labor and came together to vote on provisions and ultimately on the whole document, in confidential settings. Those who seek transparency in public oriented negotiations would regard the American negotiation process as "second best." But, even with its Civil War and now 27 amendments, the American constitution has proven to be a more robust and longer lasting negotiated agreement. Why? Negotiations in private sessions allow more trades where

Table 3. Modes of conflict resolution

MODE OF DISCOURSE	PRINCIPLED (REASONS)	BARGAINING (INTERESTS)	PASSIONS (NEEDS/ EMOTIONS/ RELIGION)
FORMS OF PROCESS:			
Closed	Some court proceedings; arbitration	Negotiation–US constitution; diplomacy	Mediation (e.g. divorce)
Open	French constitution; courts; arbitration	Public negotiations; Some labor	Dialogue movement
Plenary	French constitution	Reg-Neg	Town meetings
Committees	Faculty committees; task groups	US constitution/US Congress	Caucuses—interest groups
Expert/Facilitator	Consensus building	Mini-trial	Public conversations
Naturalistic (Leaderless)			Grass roots organizing/WTO protests
Permanent	Government, institutions	Business organizations, unions	Religious organizations, Alcoholics Anonymous, Weight Watchers
Constitutive	UN, national constitutions	National constitutions/ professional associations	Civil justice movements, peace

Temporary/ ad hoc	*Issue organizations/social justice*	Interest groups	Yippies, New Age, vigilantes

Principles = reasons, appeals to universalism, law
Bargaining = interests, preferences, trading, compromises
Open = public or transparent meetings or proceedings
Closed = confidential, secret process or outcomes (settlements)
Plenary = full group participation, joint meetings
Committees = task groups, caucuses, parts of the whole
Expert-facilitator = led by expertise (process or substantive or both)
Naturalistic = leaderless, grass roots, ad hoc
Permanent = organizational, institutional
Constitutive = constitutional

parties can agree to change publicly committed positions, as happened in some unusual alliances at the US constitutional convention. Similarly, committee negotiations allow smaller groups to hash out deals which then can be linked to arrangements from other specialty committees. The almost daily public reports to "the people" at the French Constituent Assembly permitted more public friction (and ultimately continued partisan violence) during and after the French revolution. While we cannot attribute all of these process differences as the "cause" of robustness of the negotiated constitutions, these examples suggest that negotiation process choices do matter and affect substantive outcomes.

In Table 3 we can separate out processes with expert facilitators and those without. Many commentators, for example, suggest that the lack of success of the Occupy Wall Street political movement was that it never had "leaders" to articulate demands and specific proposals for concrete reforms. The Occupy movement would say it was deliberately attempting to create a more naturalistic, leaderless movement but it failed in sustaining itself or its demands for more economic equality. One of the ironies and challenges for democratic deliberation negotiations is this potential need for expertise in process facilitation to organize agendas, consider voting rules, and help guide negotiations for productive outcomes.

As the table illustrates, when a negotiation involves different discourses of reason (principles, laws), as well as emotions, strongly held political commitments, morals, appeals to ethics, and religious or other values (e.g. abortion rights, animal rights, migration policy), the "middle" column of "bargaining" or trading for interests and needs, which is problem-solving negotiation, may be the only way to bridge such differences to reach any kind of practical accommodation (even if only contingent).

International complex negotiation (diplomacy)

International negotiations are a special case of complex negotiations. In addition to all of the issues discussed above, there are issues of language, cultural assumptions, history, and virtually always linkage of different issues (trade, military, cultural exchanges, currency, etc.). Though many books offer advice about negotiating with "other cultures," these are often simplistic and, more often, inaccurate, making assumptions that a culture is homogeneous or monolithic. As in any business, legal, or domestic negotiation, doing research about particular parties and issues and, where needed, engaging a third-party mediator (or, indeed, an interpreter) to manage cross-national negotiations is a better approach than making assumptions about so-called cultural differences. The cultural differences literature (whether backed up by empirical anthropological and sociological work or more popular treatments) makes claims about differences in timing (precise or approximate), direct or non-direct communication styles, more homogeneous or more diverse cultures, hierarchical or egalitarian cultures, gender differences, class differences, and chains of accountability. Such negotiation advice manuals tell negotiators how to speak, what body language to use, what gifts to bring, how to say yes or no (head nodding means different things in different cultures), and even what to wear.

Experienced international negotiators, whether public diplomats or private business or legal professionals, now often constitute their own "class" of cosmopolitan negotiators. Cultural differences are more likely to be observed in approaches to negotiation (collaboration or competition) depending on the issues involved. As US Secretary of State Anthony Blinken said about US–China relations, "we will be competitive when we should be, collaborative where we can be, and adversarial when we must," noting that approaches to negotiation will vary by issues, stakes, subject, timing, and parties. Like any negotiation with agents and principals (lawyers, brokers, and diplomats), international negotiations are always engaged on many fronts and layers simultaneously, with allies, with constituencies, with political parties and presidents/premiers, and, of course, opponents.

Chapter 7
Ethical and legal issues in negotiation: Making enforceable agreements

What do we owe others and how should we treat them in negotiations? This chapter explores the ethical and legal issues in making good and enforceable agreements. Ethical issues include large "*macro*" issues—judging the ends or goals of negotiation and when we should negotiate and when not. When is it morally permissible or a good idea to compromise? How do we evaluate whether we have done the right thing in the outcomes we reach for those involved in the negotiation, but also for those affected by what we do who are not at the bargaining table? Negotiations also involve judgments about the behaviors we choose, the means of negotiation—the "*micro*" choices we make before, during, and after negotiating. Negotiations have ethical consequences in what they accomplish, but also in the processes that are used to reach an agreement. Whether an agreement from a negotiation is enforceable depends on legal requirements. When negotiated agreements are not adhered to, parties may sue, declare war, or take actions of reprisals and revenge, or engage in forgiveness or restraint, or enter into a new negotiation to solve the problem of breach and make a new agreement.

To negotiate or not negotiate?

The first ethical dilemma we face in any negotiation is should we engage at all? What are we trying to accomplish with whom?

Should we bargain with someone like Hitler? The Taliban? A regime like apartheid or a colonial power? Our enemies? A businessperson who has a reputation for reneging on agreements? These questions are raised when either we think the other party is evil, not to be trusted, or the circumstances should not permit anything short of principled solutions, not negotiated compromise. The most common case study in modern negotiation theory is the dilemma of Chamberlain at Munich. Should Chamberlain have engaged at all? Why was he so accommodating, giving up the sovereignty of third-party Czechoslovakia? We study this now with a form of *hindsight bias*. John F. Kennedy, during the Cuban Missile Crisis of 1962, is often juxtaposed as a different example—testing Khrushchev's resolve by issuing a bellicose threat and sea blockade. The United States claims "never" to negotiate with hostage takers, but does it? (Think about the release of US hostages in Iran in 1979, mediated by Algerians.) These, and other similar case studies of brinkmanship diplomatic, political, hostage-taking, and military negotiations may be limited in their value for our more everyday negotiations.

How should we measure both the ethics and the efficacy of Chamberlain's negotiations with Hitler? What other options were available *at the time*? In ethics terms, do we focus on obligations, what is just and right (deontology), or what is expedient, efficient, and more utilitarian, along with the effects of our choices on ourselves and others (consequentialist)? How do we consider short-term conditions (peace now and time to prepare for later war) in relation to long-term consequences (would stronger action at Munich have prevented war)?

Despite the importance of history, we may focus too much on vivid prior cases. Recall the approach that President George H. W. Bush took after the Iraqi invasion of Kuwait because the costs of the Vietnam war were too prominently on the minds of Americans. Nelson Mandela famously absolved his own jailers by negotiating slowly over his release and the end of apartheid by focusing more on the future, rather than revenge and a possible civil war for injustices of the past. These, and many other vivid examples, are instructive, but context matters. When we use analogical thinking to decide whether to bargain with an evil regime or person are we conjuring up Hitler or our political foes? What exactly is evil about the negotiator or his regime? What facts seem the same? Which are different? Do the defeats of Napoleon and Hitler in Russia demonstrate valid analogies (can you win a military engagement in the snow with which the Russians are more familiar?). This is what George Washington did at Valley Forge (in the snow) to the British as well—the weather matters for war, less so for indoor negotiations, where different aspects of place may matter. Which facts and conditions are most relevant in deciding whether to engage and how?

Process matters. Perhaps the most controversial principle of all negotiation theory is that we hope that as long as we are still talking, we are not killing (or losing). If we are talking to someone in a negotiation they probably need something from us as much as we need something from them and staying in the negotiation may itself reveal more about what is at stake for both parties. Engagement might be useful for information gathering even if we ultimately choose not to make an agreement.

Consider the most important issue of analysis as the *"baseline"*— what happens if we do nothing? What is the status quo? Can the evil regime or person continue to do harm or grab more assets, or is there some possible intervention that could improve things?

Are there alternatives to negotiation? Must we engage with this particular negotiation partner? What might we need from the evil person or regime? How can we get it? If not directly, what is available indirectly? While we are judging the morality of a particular negotiation, what is the comparative morality of the alternatives from which we are choosing?

What is possible in difficult situations? Is some kind of opening, a first step, yes, even a compromise possible? When is incrementalism better than grandiose absolute judgments about engagement? Are there circumstances in which we should not engage at all? In our study of contexts, here it is important to remember "never say never" and "never say always."

Will any agreements reached actually be adhered to? Will a negotiated agreement make things better or worse? When does dealing with bad people or remaining in evil regimes to curb their atrocities become complicity in evil actions?

Compromise or not?

For those who seek "pure" outcomes in a negotiation, almost any compromise can seem like a loss of principle. Compromise appears to connote a "giving up" of something—a "split the difference" move to the " middle" of a set of contested possibilities. But compromise has a morality of its own. Without negotiation and compromise we could accomplish almost nothing as human beings, including legislation, international peace treaties, sales agreements, family vacations, dispute settlements, and public policy. Compromise itself has moral worth, much overlooked in philosophy, ethics, and negotiation.

To many, it seems as if giving something up is losing one's integrity, soul, or conception of self, especially if some principle is involved. But what about the other party? Sometimes agreeing to negotiate with someone actually endows another human being with equal worth and respect. Consider the role of relationship in the third model of negotiation (Chapter 2) when the relationship may be more important than what is being negotiated. Reaching an agreement may turn out to be more important than a particular principle. Compromise itself may be intrinsically valuable because it allows actions to be taken (legislation, peace agreements, transactions). As leaders from Machiavelli to Martin

Luther King and Nelson Mandela, as practical politicians, have said, it may be necessary to work incrementally with compromises among conflicting parties, in order to attain a larger goal later. Of course, all compromises must be measured temporally—what seems like a good compromise now (Munich) might seem wrong later, as many think the appeal to compromise lengthens the time to achievement of real gains. The framers of the United States constitution used many compromises to forge their governing document, including the continued recognition of slavery and anti-democratic election procedures (the Senate and the Electoral College), but *at the time* these compromises were considered by many to be superior to the alternatives, which would have meant no unified nation, potentially further chaos, both for the citizens and the finances of the new country, but with great costs to third parties not at the table—enslaved human beings.

Compromise is also seen as unprincipled when parties simply "split the difference" or use arbitrary values just to reach agreement. Split the difference settlements are often efficient, especially when, after long bargaining, there remains a close but stubborn gap in the ZOPA. A compromise can be a gesture of good faith to reach agreement. Compromise is an offer to move closer to the other party, but it is still possible to argue for a principled allocation of values based on something other than a 50–50 split. Remember that when King Solomon offered to "split the baby" in half for two contesting claims of motherhood, the real mother offered to "give up" her half in order to spare the child's life. Sometimes you have to offer to give something up to get something greater in return.

Compromise, like all negotiated agreements, must still be morally evaluated by whether it was consensual. Coercion, duress, and extreme power imbalances are morally problematic. So we may consider it immoral, unethical, or unfair when we see a compromise where one party is much more powerful (enshrined in the law by some prohibitions on "contracts of adhesion"). Compromise may seem immoral, but for those who agree to it, it might, in some cases, save a life. Context matters. What would you do to save the life of your child? Your partner? Yourself? Others?

In some settings, compromise is a positive good. Consider the gridlocked polities of many modern Western democracies. One-party rule may be more efficient and "effective" at getting things done, but those of us who believe in democracy prefer debate and deliberation. Too much deliberation can also lead to inaction. But as politicians adhere to rigid party lines and "principles" we may accomplish nothing. Political scientists argue for more compromise to demonstrate that those with different views might still engage with each other with mutual respect and good faith to meet in some zone of agreement in order to accomplish something important for the public good. Framing proposals that will appeal to more than just one side of the political divide is more likely to lead to success.

Finally, compromise can be a more "precise" justice or outcome in negotiation when it accurately reflects the interests of the parties. After many years of contested child custody disputes in the United States, some states began to recognize the legal concept of "joint custody" where children could live with and be governed by divorcing parents (alternating homes), with equal parental rights, rather than "splitting the baby" (putting child development above the claims of each parent). Such compromise solutions might be especially appropriate when legal principles or arguments are balanced or two or more parties have equally valid claims or they simply seek to minimize the damage or transaction costs of prolonged conflict.

Negotiate for and with whom? Agents in negotiation

Often we cannot choose our negotiation partners. A seller offers something we want or someone approaches us when we want to sell. Countries have border or trade disputes with each other. We have a dispute and choose to negotiate before or after we file a lawsuit or a lawsuit is filed against us. Sometimes we can choose with whom we negotiate—seeking to create a business relationship or forming a new organization or writing an ante-nuptial agreement with someone we are about to marry. In many cases we might choose a representative to negotiate for us—a lawyer, a broker, or agent—and so might the other side. Should we choose someone with a tough and adversarial reputation? Should we look for a creative problem solver? Should we learn about our counterparts' or representatives' reputations for fair dealing or hard bargaining with others? Some law firms have particular reputations, as do individuals; and consider national leaders who have tried to cultivate particular images as "tough" or "diplomatic" or "conciliatory." So, our choice of negotiation partners implicates both their behaviors and our own. In law, the principles of agency law affect what behaviors of the principal or the agent can be attributed to the other and what authorization a principal has to give her agent to act for her.

Who we choose is both a strategic decision and an ethical one. What will this agent do on our behalf? If we are the agent/lawyer/ broker how far will we go on behalf of our clients? Lawyers are told to "zealously" represent their clients—a special form of "role morality" that may allow them to do things for their clients they might not (personally) do for themselves. Lawyers must keep client communications confidential, without client permission to release, so they may not be free to share everything with negotiation counterparts. What happens when individuals or professionals from different backgrounds or different professional rules (some professions have formal ethical and disciplinary rules about negotiation behavior) come together to negotiate? Knowing the specifics of required ethical rules or legal disclosures (e.g. conditions of property, health conditions) is essential for considering who negotiates with whom and what they can ethically and legally do.

What, if anything, do negotiators owe people who are not at the negotiation table but who are affected by whatever agreements are reached: children in divorce, future generations in environmental treaties, employees of merged companies, or citizens of own and other countries? This is a philosophical question, not one answered (yet) by law, except in very limited situations (in American class action settlements lawyers must give notice and some information to those who may be affected by a legal settlement). Should a negotiator be ethically accountable to anyone affected by a negotiation? Is there any duty to be fair to others?

Behavioral issues in negotiation—what may I do versus what should I do?

In assessing actions in negotiation, it is useful to separate out questions of what we might be able to do for strategic advantages, what we are legally able to do, and what we *should* do from a moral perspective. Sources of judgment include the mirror we hold up to ourselves at day's end, our religious training, our parents, our work partners, a video of what we do, the other parties affected by what we do, the media, and eventually a court of law.

Should we make our own choices or calibrate what we do reflexively, based on what our counterparts do, or what our clients expect of us? Does context matter or do we have "golden rules" of negotiation behavior to be used in any situation?

Scholars of negotiation have classified several types of negotiators as those who (1) always maximize their gain and see the rules of negotiation as a "game" to be played, with the assumption that others are engaged in the same game and know its (implicit or explicit) rules; (2) are "idealists" who will do the "right" thing, even if it hurts themselves or their client, in order to maintain personal integrity; or (3) are "pragmatists" who conform to particular industry norms, knowing that what they do will be known by others and will likely affect what they can get away with. Some empirical studies (mostly from laboratory studies, but a few from self-reports from actual negotiations and only a few from observational studies) now document that a general culture of competition in many kinds of negotiation does encourage various forms of lying, deception, or taking advantage of other parties.

One of the greatest difficulties in assessing what happens in a negotiation is the fact that most negotiations are conducted privately. This has been used to prevent the development of more formal rules of ethical behavior in most negotiations because there is no simple way to observe and then enforce particular behaviors. In most cases our behavioral choices are ours to make with very little discipline from the outside world (except for efforts to legally void an agreement). Unethical behavior, when extreme, can cause an agreement to be voided for fraud, duress, or coercion. Agreements may also be resisted and not complied with if the parties are resentful of unfair arrangements. So, consideration of good behavior in a negotiation is both deontological (am I a good person?), as well as instrumental (can I get away with this, will this lead to a good result?). Perhaps the greatest monitor of ethical behavior in negotiation is reputation. How truthful, reliable, fair, and trustworthy a negotiator is in each encounter may affect how others approach and deal with each other.

Truth-telling, lying, deception, misrepresentation

Everyone knows that people exaggerate or "puff" when they negotiate. They ask for more than they would settle for and they offer less than they would be willing to pay. They often exaggerate the quality of an item they are selling or profess that all they have is the money in their pocket with which to buy. In the United States parties even "misrepresent" who they really are—large organizations have been known to use "strawmen" (differently named subsidiaries) when buying property because they know prices will be higher if the sellers know their true identity. Negotiation is about information and parties almost always ask each other questions: about the value of items, about the facts of the situation (past, present, and predicted future), about what they hope to accomplish in a negotiation, and to what they will agree. Are we required to tell the truth in negotiation?

Many philosophers argue that we must virtually always tell the truth. Truth connotes trust and respect in one's fellow human beings, and recognizes the value and autonomy of each individual with whom we deal; transparency is necessary in all public decision making, just allocation of resources requires knowledge of where they are, and general societal health requires knowing that people conduct themselves honestly, both in public and in private. Though philosophers weigh some of the important exceptions (a lie is permissible to save a life, as when someone holding a gun asks you where your child is, for self-defense, for keeping information about a terminal disease from some patients, or not telling the "whole truth" when asked for an opinion about one's partner's appearance), a duty-bound conception of truth telling suggests that we should have norms that encourage truth telling for societal reasons beyond the particular negotiation. Others argue that negotiation has created its own "culture" with different expectations of truth telling.

The "law" of negotiation lies somewhere in between the poles of total truth telling and expected deception. For example, in the American rules of ethics for lawyers, Rule 4.1 Model Rules of Professional Responsibility (rules for which lawyers may be disciplined) formally states that a lawyer "may not make a false statement of material fact or law to a third person." However, in formal commentary to this rule legal negotiators are permitted to not be totally truthful about things which are not "facts." The comment states that "*under generally accepted conventions* in negotiation, certain types of statements ordinarily are not taken as statements of material fact. Estimates of price or value placed on the subject of a transaction and a party's intention as to an acceptable settlement of a claim are in this category and so is the existence of an undisclosed principal except where non-disclosure of the principal would constitute fraud." With a few exceptions, the comment also suggests that there is no "affirmative duty to disclose facts." This comment seems to accept an empirical claim that negotiators will not tell the whole truth about the offers they make, the value they place on items of negotiation, whether they will accept a particular offer, or on whose behalf they are negotiating. Efforts by negotiation scholars and ethicists to eliminate this comment and make the rule a clear one of no tolerance for misrepresentations have failed for decades, demonstrating the power of professions accustomed to conventions of some deception to maintain their own norms. Among the arguments against any change in this state of affairs was that lawyers could not be held to stronger truth-telling duties than other professionals or lay negotiators as that would hinder their professional powers, in competition with other professionals (estate agents, brokers, etc.).

Deception, misrepresentation, and lies come in many forms in negotiation—"puffing," intentionally false claims of quality, value, omissions of material truths, failure to respond honestly to questions asked, partially truthful, but incomplete statements, and deflections of intent, motives, or values placed on negotiated items. To the conventional negotiator the norms of behavior may be "caveat emptor" (let the buyer beware). More practically, the buyer should do their homework to learn the true value of things; it is not the seller's duty to reveal all.

Unfortunately for the negotiator, what truth must be told varies by industry, context, and the laws of particular jurisdictions. In Anglo-American legal systems what must be truthfully disclosed in any negotiation will depend on both the common law of fraud and misrepresentation, as well as some tort and contract rules. In addition, there are now many laws (by statute) requiring mandatory disclosures in particular settings, such as housing (disclosures of known defects), some consumer items, securities and stock sales, political office disclosures, taxation, and some health conditions. These formal legal requirements, which vary in different legal systems, are quite complex in federal systems (US, Canada, Australia, Germany), where there might be different legal rules by state, province, or Länder. For example, in some jurisdictions, fraud (which can be used to void a contract) consists solely of affirmatively made misrepresentations with intent to deceive. In other jurisdictions omissions or non-disclosures of material facts, such as the condition of a roof on a house, may constitute fraud or negligent misrepresentation. Trickier is the issue of what happens when one party in a negotiation asks the other a question about a material fact and that question is deflected (not answered). Is that an intentional omission or a negligent one? That is the kind of factual and legal question on which lawsuits and liabilities turn.

Even in legal rules with such clear wording as "material facts" there are vast differences in interpretations. Is the existence of other offers a material fact? For many years a major merger and acquisitions negotiator argued that if asked if his companies had "other suitors" he would almost always say yes, indeed often suggesting there was another buyer on the doorstep, even if no firm offers had been made. Is that a "material" misrepresentation? His view was that in major deals the buyer had the responsibility to research the economic value of the company it was buying, which should be extrinsic to any other existing offer. Others (including economists, as well as ethicists) would say that the value of a company (or a house or furniture at an antiques market) is affected by additional offers. Market prices are affected by what others value, so a suggestion that there are offers is "material" to valuation judgments. Consider the situation in which a seller placed an expensive flat on the market. He then invited several friends to attend the open house to feign enthusiasm and to loudly state they were going to bid on the flat (in high numbers). Seeing the enthusiasm of these "shills," a purchaser bid more on the flat and was successful in obtaining the contract (at over the asking price). When the purchaser later learned what had happened he was able to legally reverse the sale as at least one court treated this as fraudulent price manipulation.

A large body of behavioral research has documented that most of us think we are more ethical than we are and that the other side is less ethical than we are. These are called ethical "blind spots" in negotiation and can affect how we process information cognitively (whom do we trust) and justify to ourselves (motivational biases) when we think we are "responding" appropriately to a "liar" or a "cheat" on the other side. Or we are just using the "generally accepted conventions" to justify our own less than forthcoming behavior.

Thus, important things to do in all negotiations are ask a lot of questions and investigate facts, personnel, and conditions. Asking questions persistently and demanding answers, in writing where possible, is one way to protect against deception, or at least to get it on the record.

Other unethical tactics, tricks, and concerns of hard bargaining

Although misrepresentations, puffing, bluffing, and lying are the most obviously common ethically questioned activities, many negotiators engage in some of the hard bargaining techniques and dirty tricks noted in Chapter 4. Empirical research demonstrates that there is a great variation in the use or acceptability of these tactics by industry, profession, and gender (women are less likely to engage in these practices). Some professions attempt to proscribe some of this behavior in ethical codes. The dilemmas for any negotiator are (1) whether to engage in any of these practices; (2) how to respond if they are used against you; and (3) whether to report them or (4) try to change the (ethical) culture of negotiation.

Are these tactics effective? Does it matter whether a client or principal has authorized them in an agent-based negotiation? Could they be used to void a deal or cause resistance to compliance with the agreement? Might they lead to some adverse consequences like disbarment, discipline, or voiding of the contract? What reputation is created by engaging in such behaviors?

There are protections against some of these tactics. "A tactic understood is no tactic" is a good maxim. So all negotiators, whether game players, idealists, or pragmatists, should at least learn about these tactics and consider appropriate responses. One effective tool is to explicitly question or call out what is being done (e.g. "Are you calling me at 5 pm on Friday to instill a sense of emergency and false deadline? Let's talk after the weekend"). My own personal favorite is to explicitly say, "Do you really mean to say or do X?..." (demonstrating that I know how I am being manipulated). More preparation and time-outs are always advised when a negotiator feels boxed in and may need to regroup or seek allies or more information away from the bargaining table. Direct talk and more specific questions, with persistence, are important tools for "turning" the conversation to greater specificity rather than using power moves. At a more technical level, negotiators can ask for warranties, guarantees, contingent agreements, with conditions, and formal clauses in written agreements (requiring more honest disclosures backed up with possible legal remedies).

Ultimately, we know that not all negotiators share the same moral compass and that behaviors will vary by situation and person, but knowing one's own moral limits and being prepared to deal with those of others is necessary for negotiators.

Fairness and good faith

The objective of any negotiation is to come to an agreement. Should negotiators bear any responsibility for the fairness of any agreement they reach? Diplomatic negotiators think about the effects of their agreements on their own country and by necessity often have to think about the consequences for others to ensure compliance with the agreement. The Treaty of Versailles ending World War I is considered a negotiation dominated by the victors, leaving the losers (Germany) ready to disregard the treaty, rearm, and seek revenge. Parents negotiating a divorce must consider how fair their agreement is not only to each other but also to their children. Those negotiating environmental agreements explicitly see themselves as negotiating better climate, resource usage, and conditions for future generations who are not at the bargaining table. Those negotiating complex mergers and acquisitions must consider how their deals will impact not only the shareholders, but employees, customers, and even the general public (and the government if it is scrutinizing competitive practices). Instrumentally, all negotiators should take account of whether an agreement is at least fair enough to ensure compliance with its terms.

Fairness is an elusive concept, both philosophically and practically. When we ask what is fair or just we may be looking at substantive fairness, including distributive fairness (are parties getting a rightful share), equity, equality, and procedural fairness (was a good faith and transparent process used).

Some suggest that negotiated agreements should be measured by the rules of law that provide clear legal endowments and expressions of what the formal law would consider a just agreement. But to most negotiation scholars and practitioners, fairness is a different concept. As long as an agreement is not otherwise unlawful, the parties may agree to use their own definition of fairness—what seems right or at least accomplishable in their particular case. Negotiated matters are often intended to be particularized agreements for the parties (consented to by them) rather than legal rules which have been created for the "general public." In many settings professional negotiators will use such concepts as "the law of the shop" (labor law), "reasonable commercial practices" (sales law), what is customary (who pays for wandering cattle grazing), or the "going rate" of a particular commodity. These are concepts of fairness, sometimes negotiated over decades or centuries to capture understandings of fairness in particular markets or communities. Some negotiated agreements are measured by legal standards in contract law principles or international law, but many negotiations are subject to their own internal conceptions of fairness.

The law of enforceable negotiations—contract, defenses, fraud, misrepresentation, unconscionability, breach, international law

When a negotiation is completed it creates an agreement or contract. Depending on the legal jurisdiction and subject matter, this agreement can be oral, consummated by a handshake, or documented in writing, notarized by a witness or official, and, in some cases, still subject to ratification by others (principals, trade union members, officers of companies, legislatures, or countries). Some negotiations have to meet certain formalities to be fully valid, such as international treaties which require a specified number of countries to agree before the treaty enters into full force.

Most written negotiated agreements are contracts, subject to the legal contract rules in the relevant jurisdiction. In common law countries this means an offer, an acceptance, and some exchange of value (called "consideration"). In most civil law countries an exchange of promises is sufficient under the applicable civil code provisions. After a contract is signed, either it is performed as specified, or there may be a breach of the agreement which may result in a lawsuit by the party seeking to enforce the agreement or by the party seeking to be relieved of performance. Most legal systems allow certain defenses to the enforcement of a contract. Contracts that have been reached by coercion, duress, undue influence, lack of capacity, mistake, misrepresentation, fraud, or certain other bad behaviors during the negotiation may result in a court finding the contract invalid. Most jurisdictions, both civil and common law, also have some form of the unconscionability doctrine—a court may have discretion to void an agreement which is grossly unfair, either because of substantive terms (too one-sided) or procedural unconscionability (a process unfairly dominated by one party). These are rarely successful claims but there is increasing attention to such "contracts of adhesion" where there is little negotiation about specific terms. The European Union and some other jurisdictions now have consumer protection laws which may void particular contracts, assumed to be not freely negotiated, but the online world presents some new difficulties in assessing fairness in negotiations. There are other contract doctrines which can affect the enforcement of negotiated agreements such as *force majeure* or impossibility of performance, witnessed in the Covid-19 pandemic when many negotiated contracts could not be performed due to cessation of business and travel, and mandatory closures. Many courts will have to consider how to allocate losses and risks where there are no clear contingency, exclusion, warranty, or *force majeure* clauses in the agreements. Not only must good negotiators draft a good legal agreement, they must also be a futurist troubleshooter, anticipating possible problems and future risks. The best agreements always both consider contingency clauses and provide for dispute resolution clauses—how the parties will renegotiate or resolve any new disputes that arise from the agreement.

Chapter 8
The future of negotiation

The process of negotiating with others is essential to the satisfaction of so many human needs. How we negotiate is changing and adapting to the future—online, electronic negotiations, hybridization of different kinds of negotiation and dispute resolution processes, and new forms of communication are employed to make negotiation more accessible to everyone, but also more complex, as we engage in so many cross-cultural negotiations. One question for the future is which of the several frameworks we have focused on will dominate our thinking and behavior. Will we be creative problem solvers or competitors for increased scarcity as we face the challenges of international commerce, climate change, limited resources, cultural exchange, and domestic and international conflicts?

New forms of negotiation: Electronic and virtual negotiation

How much negotiation was there in your last purchase? Did you go into a shop or buy something online? In many Western cultures, outside of informal street markets, we are used to having listed prices, with little to no negotiation. But in many countries purchases are negotiated (automobiles, secondhand goods, art, jewelry, and, almost worldwide, food in markets). Increasingly our purchases are conducted through internet platforms (at the time of this writing about 21 percent of all commerce, up from 5 percent in 2007, and 11 percent in 2015). Some sites like eBay or Alibaba manage auctions or bidding where there is bargaining between anonymous purchasers and sellers. Other sites permit negotiations in text boxes allowing a little more room for discursive and principled offers. Much of this commerce moves automatically without human intervention, until there is a problem and a need for a return, refund, or customer service. eBay was the first company to offer mass and efficient ODR in which those with complaints about their purchases could deal directly with each other online and then later appeal to an online mediator. Some customer services now provide hybrid forms of negotiation and dispute resolution which begin in automatic tick-boxes but can also move to human Ombuds. Online negotiation, utilized by both private and public entities, can reduce claims to arguments that fit into predetermined categories or are responded to automatically, reducing the ability to make tailored appeals for good negotiated solutions.

Despite its limitations, this form of interaction, without face-to-face encounters, can be very efficient, using algorithms, artificial intelligence, and machine learning (e.g. "if the complaint is under $50.00 and this is a first-time complaint, just refund the money"). No need to negotiate anything. This form of "digital negotiation" raises important questions about fairness. Will repeat purchasers with big accounts get better treatment, based on how algorithms are programmed? Will those with computer literacy and patience do better?

Modern rating services (e.g. Yelp, Trip Advisor) permit some public redress by allowing complaints publicly (and then having vendors make offers to take down bad references) and by allowing aggregation of complaints when others see they are not alone. Social media and more public demands also permit crowdsourced potential solutions, thus expanding the idea pool for more creative problem solving. However, such forms of public negotiating may also falsely damage reputations and lead to more disputes about who is right without any adjudication.

Some legal jurisdictions, like the European Union, have begun to develop formal methods for ODR and negotiation of sales of goods, primarily in the consumer goods spheres (EU Regulation 524/2013). Many countries now use online Ombuds services to negotiate and settle or otherwise adjudicate disputes with public utilities, banks, energy providers, retail, communications, transportation, and other public services or private entities.

Legal rules about what constitutes a contract or a breach or what remedies might be available are being modified by law and practice. In some jurisdictions, courts (especially for smaller claims) are moving online completely (United Kingdom, parts of Canada, US, and Australia) with implications for how we exercise legal rights. Some have claimed there will be less need for lawyers and other agents as more and more people negotiate directly. Zoom and other interactive platforms permit some hybrid of interactive computer-assisted negotiation and individual personalized dispute resolution. During the Covid pandemic some forms of negotiation were made easier (and cheaper) this way—no need to travel to a central meeting location. Early uses of online negotiation for dispute resolution included computerized "third-party" settlement services, such as Cybersettle, in which parties engaged in a dispute entered offers to settle into a computer space which then allowed three attempts to match a ZOPA. The idea was that allowing three attempts would lead to some learning about each party's "limits" and "demands." In its earliest form this type of automated computer-assisted negotiation reduced all negotiations to monetary claims. Now it is possible to negotiate about numbers in a bargaining range but also to produce text-based, more complex tailored offers and proposals.

The question of whether creative, tailored solutions to negotiable problems will be enhanced or limited by these new forms of communication remains to be answered. Some will always prefer face-to-face communications; others will prefer more anonymity. New electronic forms of negotiation permit both synchronous and asynchronous communication, allowing more time for possible reflection, research, and idea generation, as well as more "cooling down" of more conflictual encounters. However, some research on online communication suggests that some people can more easily escalate conflict (called "flame mail") when they are not in the same room as their counterparts.

Hybrid forms of negotiation and dispute resolution

Basic two-party negotiation is the foundation for most human dispute resolution and contracting. Having learned the basics here (frameworks of orientation, analysis of stakes and interests, key concepts of ZOPA, BATNA, reservation prices, behavioral choices, first offers, principles, concession patterns, brainstorming, creative problem solving) and ethical and legal principles for enforcement of agreement, we have observed how negotiation becomes more complex as more parties and more issues are added. Now we have added virtual online negotiations, but also large meetings of delegations for multi-party complex diplomatic negotiations conducted over long periods of time. Consider all the locations and time spent to negotiate the Iran Nuclear Agreement, which involved the five members of the UN Security Council and Germany, as well as the European Union.

Many international negotiations have consisted of formal talks at a public diplomatic table (Track One diplomacy), but many modern international negotiations have also had more private side negotiations (Track Two), including the Vietnam–US Paris Peace Accords (1973), the US–Iran Hostage Negotiations (1979–80) where secondary officials used trial balloons and suggestions to see what might be possible before anything was formally proposed. The Israeli–Palestinian Oslo Accords (1993, 1995) employed yet another form of diplomatic negotiation (beyond Track Two)—informal talks by academics, and mid-level non-governmental civil society negotiators, meeting totally in secret, without full government authorization, to see what was possible. These are generically called "problem-solving workshops."

We have seen mediation used in international negotiations, including Northern Ireland, Bosnia-Herzegovina, and the Middle East. Mediators see themselves as "adding value" to negotiations, whether facilitating communication, proposing their own ideas, or using a "one-text" process to neutralize the "reactive devaluation" that comes from direct party negotiations or separate "shuttle diplomacy" (caucus) meetings. These additions to two-party negotiations by employing a third-party negotiation facilitator, mediator, process manager, or consensus builder are now used in virtually every other form of human negotiation, from commercial disputes, to the negotiation of mergers and acquisitions, to construction projects, to family disputes, and in criminal matters, with the use of victim–offender mediation.

Negotiation and dispute resolution experts are now part of a new field, called Dispute System Design, in which they help parties planning a new venture or in conflict to develop a process that is suited to their particular matter. The South African Truth and Reconciliation Commission is an illustration of how a sophisticated process was developed to allow for direct communication between victims, survivors, and perpetrators of the apartheid regime, seeking truth, apologies, forgiveness, accountability, and some amnesty. In large-scale construction projects (bridges, roads, buildings, and dams) in the United States there is "partnering" where all the contractors, architects, sub-contractors, and future users gather in advance to negotiate not only the terms of a contract but also the terms of their relationships and processes for resolving disputes during the life of the project.

Negotiation professionals now plan in advance, draft contract clauses and processes (called "tiers" (vertical) or "menus" (horizontal) of dispute processes), and then manage direct negotiations, mediation, and sometimes hybrid forms like mediation-arbitration (med-arb) or arb-med, in which facilitated negotiation processes are supplemented with third-party decisions and process management. Modern international treaties now also provide for a hierarchy (tiers) or choice (menu) of dispute processes, including direct negotiation, then assisted negotiation, fact finding, conciliation, mediation, arbitration, and then, if all else fails, some decisional tribunal.

Private and public entities, including the United Nations, World Bank, multinational corporations, government agencies, universities, and other large organizations, have also adapted negotiation processes for the resolution of internal organizational disputes, such as employment and quality of service or product issues. Internal dispute systems (called Internal Dispute Resolution—IDR) or Ombuds services require direct negotiation between disputing parties as a condition precedent to the use of other processes. These processes can be cost efficient and allow for remedies which are more tailored to parties' needs (such as transfers, replacement goods, etc.) and are more future-focused than more traditional legal remedies.

New models of negotiation are used in formal governmental and public policy processes as well. In the United States, a new process of "reg-neg" (negotiated rule making) brings together all of the stakeholders in various areas of regulation (occupational health and safety, environment, indigenous affairs, land use, health care policy, transportation policy) to negotiate regulatory standards, in advance of rule promulgation by governmental authorities. The concept is that openly negotiated arguments about the impact of particular rules will allow a more consensually accepted set of regulations, with more compliance and less after-the-fact contention in litigation. Such public policy negotiations can take the form of informal Town Hall meetings or formally managed negotiated public meetings, with the possibility of formal rules following votes as in local zoning and land use issues in many American cities. In some periods of extreme political conflict such processes have been attempted to ameliorate political gridlock. In the 1990s a group of legislators from both political parties in the United States Congress met at a retreat to see if they could negotiate new rules and practices of civility. This lasted for only a short period of time but is regularly suggested in what are now even more conflictual political times.

In many countries parties filing lawsuits against each other are now required to engage in negotiation before they can proceed to a court hearing. Court systems throughout the world, including both civil law and common law countries, now often require a mandatory settlement conference for negotiation between the parties, often facilitated by a magistrate or judge.

Challenges to negotiation in the future: Global conflict in resource and political competition

Despite the fact that negotiation is now widely taught in law, business, public policy, international relations, and primary and secondary schools (and in specialized conflict resolution programs), the general public still often defaults (depending on the larger culture) to traditional competitive assumptions of scarcity and adversarial behaviors.

Although many negotiation professionals and diplomats have created a culture of their own in seeking multilateral, creative problem-solving and peace-seeking alternatives to adversarial and scarcity assumptions, there is a continuing challenge in the commitment of some political leaders to hard stances on trade and other geopolitical and economic issues. Furthermore, the ongoing climate change crisis and competition over resources such as clean water, air, and energy and some border disputes pose the ultimate challenge of whether nation-states will collaborate to solve such problems or engage in bellicose relations, physical conflict, and new styles of war (cyberwar, known as "grey war"). Are we heading to a new "cold war" of bilateral economic and political competition of China vs the West, less regional cooperation (Brexit), with many points of conflict, which could enable new models to emerge, with more complex multilateral engagement? Or is global competition just heating up on more fronts with more issues?

As we began this book with introductions to different "frames" through which to analyze negotiation problems, world leaders now face these issues every day—a global Prisoner's Dilemma. Do we collaborate/cooperate or compete/defect in working with others to search for new solutions (e.g. new energy sources, economic specialization, medical and scientific collaborations, de-nuclearization, migration) or attempt to maximize national gain? One could draw a map of trouble spots in the world: see *Council on Foreign Relations, Global Conflict Tracker* (Kashmir, Syria, North Korea, Afghanistan, US–China, US–Iran, Israel–Palestine) or resource conflicts (the Nile, Indus, Colorado, and Amazon rivers) or air pollution and try to imagine how these situations should be negotiated with different negotiation frameworks. Every day the headlines present an array of negotiation problems to solve—at both process and substantive levels.

Culture and conflict

We have emphasized that context matters in all negotiations. Yet there is an issue common to all negotiations—how should negotiators approach each other? As opponent, competitor, partner, or counterpart? The orientation to our counterparts is determined by what we are negotiating about and who we and "they" are. Each of us belongs to national, ethnic, gendered, class, religious, and political cultures and we have belief systems and also are usually situated in a role (buyer, seller, lawyer, broker, client, government official, labor representative, partner, parent, employee, manager, diplomat) which often constrains how we analyze and behave in negotiation settings. But can we create a culture of negotiation that may help us to transcend some of these cultural differences to work toward productive, not necessarily competitive, outcomes? As negotiation analyst Deepak Malhotra likes to say, "every problem wants to be solved." How we do so requires us to ask both what process should be used and what substantive possibilities exist. There is a moral dimension to this question too. What, if anything, do we owe others—both those with whom we negotiate and those who are affected by what we negotiate?

Which framework? Competition or problem solving

Negotiation books are full of examples of successful and failed deals in the business world, many failed negotiations in the diplomatic world, and a greater variety of stories in interpersonal negotiations. Often these negotiation examples and stories are told as "one-off" encounters of conflict or, less often, collaboration. Representations of negotiation in popular culture, sadly, tend to emphasize the competitive and the dramatic (as in hostage taking, spy stories, wars, crimes, big business ventures, trials, and courtroom scenes) instead of more successful and more incremental and quiet, less visible problem solving (such as the Cuban Missile Crisis in *Thirteen Days* (2000), child custody in *I am Sam* (2001), prisoner exchange in *Bridge of Spies* (2015)) which might better reflect and educate the public about different ways to negotiate—promises as well as threats, collaborative solutions, resource-creating solutions, private appeals to mutual and joint interests rather than public grandstanding and bellicosity. We are beginning to see more memoirs of diplomats and public negotiators illustrating more emphasis on process and mediative negotiation approaches. As we ask in so many historical settings, can the person shape the circumstances by choosing and affecting the terms of engagement, or will the circumstances shape what the person can do?

Learning from experience?

Increasingly schoolchildren are taught to "use their words" and explore peer mediation to deal with schoolyard conflicts. Higher education students may encounter negotiation courses and concepts in psychology, political science, decision science, business, and urban planning programs. Some professional schools now mandate negotiation studies, in a recognition that "conflict resolution is the highest of all human skills," as the philosopher Stuart Hampshire has said. Families in distress go to counseling to learn how to problem solve and communicate directly about their issues. Would-be diplomats are now trained in negotiation principles and are asked to practice in role-play situations to get feedback about their choices. Negotiation analysts and theorists digest case studies, test behavioral hypotheses in social laboratories, and look for productive interventions, moves, and turns.

Those in such learning environments are asked to reflect on the interests and needs of self and others, strategies for discovering relevant and accurate information, processes for developing creative solutions to conflicts and transactions, analysis and planning for encounters with others, and techniques for negotiation evaluation of both processes and outcomes. A common feedback technique is to debrief a negotiation by asking core questions:

What went well (and why)?

What should I have done differently (and why)?

This provides a road map for thinking about negotiations in advance (see Appendix), choosing behaviors for action (after analysis), based on decades of theoretical and empirical work from a diverse set of disciplines. A good negotiator should always ask the following questions:

What is at stake in this negotiation?

What do I (my client, my country) want to accomplish and what do we value?

What do the other(s) want to accomplish and what do they value?

What are the contexts of our negotiation?

What are the limits of what we can do (laws, resources)?

What is the information I need to know about the subject of our negotiation (and what possible sources of that information are there)?

What possible (creative) solutions are there to this problem/issue/ situation?

How can we follow up and evaluate any negotiated agreement we reach for possible revision and improvement?

These questions should help us prepare for and learn from every negotiation. We should learn from all negotiations but also recognize not to learn too much—analogies can be deceptive as well as helpful. There are overarching principles and frameworks in negotiation but every encounter has its own characteristics, with personalities, cultural influences, cognitive and social biases, and the resource opportunities and limitations of particular situations. Negotiations are rich and complex. As you begin your next negotiation I hope the lessons of this book will lead to processes and outcomes that satisfy you and the other parties present or affected by your agreement.

Appendix
Negotiation plan

I. Goals, interests, and needs

   a. What are my/our/client's goals, interests, and needs?

   b. What are the goals, interests, and needs of all the other parties?

      i. Now known

      ii. To be discovered

   c. What are the possible gains/benefits of negotiating an agreement?

      i. To me/us/our client

      ii. To the other parties

   d. What are the possible losses of not negotiating an agreement?

      i. For me/us/our client

      ii. For the other parties

II. Information strategies

   a. What information do we have about the situation?

   b. What information do we need about:

      i. Facts of the situation

      ii. Other parties' goals

      iii. Our own needs, goals

      iv. Other possible agreements/deals to be made

   c. What are possible sources of that information?

      i. Public

      ii. Other party

      iii. Other?

d. What information should we share with other parties about our goals, interests, facts?

III. Context/factors affecting negotiation

    a. What is at stake?

    b. Is this a dispute negotiation (for settlement) or a deal (transactional) negotiation?

    c. Numbers of parties

    d. Numbers of issues

    e. Direct negotiation with parties or dealing with agents/lawyers/brokers?

    f. Power relations of the parties

    g. Is a longer-term relationships desired (commercial, diplomatic, personal) or not?

    h. What effects on other parties?

    i. Potential precedential effects of any agreement

    j. What effects on other people?

    k. Economic values of possible deals/agreements

    l. Political issues in making a deal (diplomatic, governmental, organizational)

    m. Psychological issues (risk preferences, effects on own psychological well-being and others)

    n. Social issues—who else affected by negotiation

    o. Cultural issues—demographics, if relevant, of negotiators

    p. Ethical/moral/religious issues of parties

    q. Need for finality—ability to renegotiate-reopen?

IV. Merits of the negotiation

    a. Can we map the possible Zone of Agreement?

    b. Assess Best Alternatives, Worst Alternatives, Most Likely Alternatives, and All possible Alternatives (BATNA, WATNA, MLATNA, and ATNA) to this possible negotiated agreement

    c. If legal dispute—what are relevant laws and legal endowments? What happens (in court or elsewhere) if agreement not achieved? Law? Facts? Other decision makers?

d. If diplomatic dispute—what are other alternatives, if any, to negotiated agreements?

e. If transactional negotiation—what other deals are possible? What are the advantages and disadvantages of this possible deal or arrangement?

f. What are the "deal points"—the things we must have to make this agreement?

g. What are the "deal killers"—what are the things which, if insisted upon by the other party, would make arrangement unacceptable?

V. Solutions/proposals/offers

a. Given our goals, interests, and needs and those we know about other parties, what possible proposals are there? (Brainstorm all possible ideas for solutions.)

b. What do we think other parties might propose?

c. What other possible sources are there for resources, expertise, and ideas for proposals?

VI. Agenda

a. What issues must be discussed in order to reach agreement?
   i. Our items
   ii. Other parties' items

b. What order of discussion?

c. Agreement on whole or by issue?

VII. Scripting

a. What proposals should we make and what reasons/rationales support them?

b. How are other parties likely to respond?

c. What proposals are other parties likely to make?

d. How should we respond?

e. If relevant, how do we map and plan our proposal/offer structure or "concession" pattern?

f. How to approach other parties?

        i. "Foreplay"

        ii. Mode of negotiation (based on what is at stake and assessment of parties):

1. Collaborative
2. Adversarial
3. Questioning-open-skeptical

        iii. Method of negotiation

1. In person
2. Telephone
3. Electronic-online
4. Other

        iv. What parties present/involved? Add, change? Subtract?

h. Rules of process/ground rules

i. Rules of decision—when is agreement reached? (Voting? Other?)

VIII. Agreement and implementation

  a. Clarification of terms

  b. Drafting/writing of agreement

  c. Necessary approvals—clients, ratifications, legal

  d. Terms of performance

      i. Payments

      ii. Warranties and guarantees, indemnities

      iii. Assessments/compliance

      iv. Remedies—renegotiation

  e. Reality testing—troubleshooting—what could go wrong? Preventive measures?

  f. Dispute resolution clauses—contingent agreements, re-negotiation, re-openers, mediation, arbitration, adjudication, other

IX. Evaluation

  a. What went well? Why?

  b. What did not go well? Why?

  c. What should have been done differently?

  d. Lessons for future negotiations

Glossary

ADR Alternative/Appropriate Dispute Resolution is the general term to reference all non-court forms of dispute resolution, including negotiation, mediation, arbitration, and their hybrids, med-arb, arb-med, consensus building, and Ombuds processes.

anchoring use of a high number or offer, or a vivid or available image or symbol (e.g. list price) early in a negotiation to frame the negotiation terrain and to set the parameters of the negotiation (see also *framing*).

aspiration point the highest aim or goal of a negotiation, set before negotiations begin. See also *target point*.

ATNA Alternatives To a Negotiated Agreement is the process of thinking about and planning for all the possibilities of alternatives to particular negotiated agreements (can include other possible negotiations with other parties, other substantive agreements; litigation, conflict, war).

authority instructions on negotiation offers and limits given to an agent in a negotiation, often governed by agent–principal rules of law, e.g. "I do not have the authority to accept that offer, as per instructions of my principal."

backward mapping a planning device for considering ultimate goals in a negotiation and then moving backward to consider all the parties and issues that should be engaged to move forward to achieve those goals; especially important in multi-party situations.

BATNA Best Alternative To a Negotiated Agreement connotes consideration of the best (away from the particular negotiation event) other solution that could be reached in order to assess whether there are better approaches to a particular negotiation, thus affecting choices about whether to stay and conclude a particular negotiation or to pursue other processes, parties, or outcomes elsewhere.

bottom line the least that one will accept in a particular negotiation before walking away; see *reservation price*, *resistance point*.

consensus building a process used in multi-party negotiations for reaching agreements by pursuing consensus (consent by "most," not necessarily unanimous, participants); usually facilitated by a third party (mediator, facilitator) to manage process of negotiation, decision rules, and deliberation rules.

Dispute System Design a process used by organizations, governments, and professionals to create procedures for iterated, repeat disputes of employees, customers, citizens, members, including *tiers* (vertical use of negotiation, mediation, Ombuds, arbitration, adjudication with designated terms and time limits) and *menus* (horizontal choice of one or another process). Used to manage individual disputes and to monitor systemic issues within an organization.

distributive bargaining negotiation with scarce resources which must be divided, e.g. assumptions of scarcity, *zero-sum gains and losses*. Assumptions of distributional issues usually produce competitive adversarial negotiation processes.

endowment effect those who have or own items tend to value them more than those who are negotiating or seeking to buy them, also known as *prospect theory* and *status quo bias*.

framing use of words, numbers, images, symbols, or metaphors to start a negotiation and control description of problem, offers, and outcomes, as in *primacy*; taking control by going first and naming the issues and terrain of negotiation.

hurting stalemate impasse, time of maximum disagreement, usually both parties suffering harm or injury (as in war of attrition); possibly time "ripe" for intervention or change of strategy.

integrative bargaining negotiation with possibility of shared, complementary, or non-conflictual interests or where it is possible to expand or increase the items being negotiated; adding value by seeking new solutions to a negotiated problem; often involves adding, rather than subtracting or narrowing, items for negotiation and trade.

intensity of negotiation number of rounds or amount of time spent negotiating. A high intensity negotiation is one with lots of communication, exchange of many offers/proposals, and possibly use of time; low intensity is only one or few rounds of offers, or a quickly concluded agreement.

landmine test for information asking questions of negotiation counterpart one already knows the answer to; seeking confirmation of trustworthiness of information offered.

linkage issues that are tied together for negotiation purposes; may or may not be related to each other, but will be perceived as affecting acceptance of both particular terms or agreement as a whole; consider pulling on thread of a spider web as a single thread affecting whole structure; see *log rolling*.

log rolling the process of trading items during a negotiation; especially used in legislative negotiations; trades may have nothing to do with each other but allow packages of proposals to be approved with different needs and interests of parties being traded to assure agreement on a bigger, multi-issue negotiation.

low balling a practice of asking for more after agreement is concluded, considered unfair by many; or a very, very low initial offer; used in both senses: see *nibbling*.

mediation facilitated negotiation; a process in which a third party assists the principal parties' negotiation by setting ground rules, monitoring communication, setting an agenda, helping find solutions, and testing and facilitating agreements, either in joint sessions or using caucuses or shuttle diplomacy.

MLATNA Most Likely Alternative To Negotiated Agreement can be used as a measuring device for consideration of what is most likely to happen if agreement is not reached (e.g. prediction of court results, more conflict, war, forbearance); helps to assist in deciding whether to continue negotiation.

nibbling a practice of demanding more after an agreement has been reached; see *low balling*; considered unfair by many.

ODR online dispute resolution is the use of any computer, internet, or electronic assistance with dispute resolution, including email negotiations, electronic customer service, Ombuds service, online platform-assisted negotiations, mediation, arbitration, and now adjudication with online courts.

Pareto optimality the point at which no party can be made better off without creating some loss to other parties; the point at which gains are maximized for all parties; can be many points in a complex agreement where everyone gets most of what is desired.

reactive devaluation the discounting of information or negotiation offers or proposals because they come from "the other side"; our inability to credit information from people in different roles; a subset of social-psychological processes of processing information by "labeling" sources of information (e.g. plaintiff-defendants; parents-children, student-teacher, etc.)

reservation price the least that one will accept in a negotiation, the "walk-away" point; see also *bottom line* and *resistance point*.

resistance point the point at which a negotiator reaches their limit and will walk away from any further negotiation; see also *bottom line* and *reservation price*.

scripting a preparation for negotiation process of planning proposals, offers, rationales, and anticipating what counterpart will offer or respond and preparing hypothetical responses, counter-offers, and other proposals with rationales.

split the difference a common compromise solution to negotiations with acceptance of offers "in the middle" of two offers.

status quo bias people value what they have or own more than what they will seek to buy or gain. Sellers value items more than buyers; people generally are risk averse for seeking gains and will prefer preventing losses of what they already have; affects valuations in negotiations.

target point hoped-for goal or high aim for negotiation; see *aspiration point*. Generally, those who aim high do better in negotiation.

WATNA Worst Alternative To Negotiated Agreement: the worst thing that could happen if a particular negotiation is not successful, e.g. loss in litigation, more conflict, war, greater loss; a motivator for staying at the negotiation table when other outcomes are bad, even if negotiated possibilities may be undesirable.

ZOPA Zone of Possible Agreement: the range of values and possible agreements that are acceptable to both sides; given target points and reservation prices this can be a large range of possible solutions, requiring allocation of surplus value, or very small. When there is no ZOPA, with no possible set of proposals or offers that parties find acceptable, there will be no agreement.

References and further reading

Chapter 1: When we need others to accomplish something

Deutsch, Morton, *The Resolution of Conflict: Constructive and Destructive Processes* (New Haven: Yale University Press 1973).

Fisher, Roger, William Ury, and Bruce Patton, *Getting to YES: Negotiating Agreement Without Giving In* (New York: Penguin, 3rd edn. 2011).

Follett, Mary Parker, *Mary Parker Follett: Prophet of Management: A Celebration of Writings from the 1920s*, Pauline Graham, ed. (Boston: Harvard Business School Press 1995).

Gulliver, P. H., *Disputes and Negotiations: A Cross-Cultural Perspective* (New York and London: Academic Press 1979).

Honeyman, Christopher and Andrea Kupfer Schneider, eds, *The Negotiator's Desk Reference* (St Paul, MN: DRI Press 2017).

Lax, David and James Sebenius, *The Manager as Negotiator: Bargaining for Cooperative and Competitive Gain* (New York: Free Press 1986).

Menkel-Meadow, Carrie, Andrea Kupfer Schneider, and Lela Love, *Negotiation: Processes for Problem Solving* (New York: Wolters Kluwer, 3rd edn 2021).

Mnookin, Robert H., *Bargaining with the Devil: When to Negotiate, When to Fight* (New York: Simon & Schuster 2010).

Mnookin, Robert, Scott Peppet, and Andrew Tulumello, *Beyond Winning: Negotiating to Create Value in Deals and Disputes* (Cambridge, MA: Harvard University Press 2000).

Raiffa, Howard, *The Art and Science of Negotiation* (Cambridge, MA: Harvard University Press 1982).

Shell, Richard, *Bargaining for Advantage: Negotiation Strategies for Reasonable People* (New York: Penguin, 2nd edn 2006).

Walton, R. E. and R. B. McKersie, *A Behavioral Theory of Labor Negotiations: An Analysis of Social Interaction System* (Ithaca, NY: Cornell University Press 1965).

Chapter 2: Frameworks of negotiation: Winning for self or problem solving for all?

Adams, James L., *Conceptual Blockbusting* (New York: Basic Books, 5th edn 2019).

Axelrod, Robert, *The Evolution of Cooperation* (New York: Basic Books 1984).

Axelrod, Robert, *The Complexity of Cooperation: Agent Based Models of Cooperation and Competition* (Princeton: Princeton University Press 1997).

Bazerman, Max and Margaret Neale, *Negotiating Rationally* (New York: Free Press 1992).

Brams, Stephen and Alan Taylor, *Fair Division: From Cake Cutting to Dispute Resolution* (New York: Cambridge University Press 1996).

Coons, John, "Compromise as Precise Justice," in *NOMOS XII Compromise in Ethics Law and Politics*, J. Roland Pennock and John Chapman, eds (New York: NYU Press 1979).

Follett, Mary Parker, "Constructive Conflict," in *Mary Parker Follett: Prophet of Management: A Celebration of Writings from the 1920's*, Pauline Graham, ed. (Boston: Harvard Business School Press 1995).

Gardner, Howard E., *Multiple Intelligences: New Horizons in Theory and Practice* (New York: Basic Books 2006).

Gutmann, Amy and Dennis Thompson, *The Spirit of Compromise: Why Governing Demands it and Campaigning Undermines it* (Princeton: Princeton University Press 2012).

Harvard Program on Negotiation Newsletter, "Government Negotiations: Pfizer's Rocky Road to U.S. Covid-19 Vaccine Deals," <https://www.pon.harvard.edu/daily/business-negotiations/government...mail&utm_medium=daily&utm_dat2021-01-25-13-30-00&mqsc=E4126136>. Jan. 25, 2021.

Lax, David and James Sebenius, *3D Negotiation: Powerful Tools to Change the Game in your Most Important Deals* (Boston: Harvard Business School Press 2006).

Margalit, Avishai, *On Compromise and Rotten Compromises* (Princeton: Princeton University Press 2010).

Menkel-Meadow, Carrie, "Toward Another View of Legal Negotiation: The Structure of Problem Solving," *UCLA Law Review* 31: 754–842 (1984).

Menkel-Meadow, Carrie, "Aha? Is Creativity Possible in Legal Problem Solving and Teachable in Legal Education?" *Harvard Negotiation Law Review* 6: 97–144 (2001).

Menkel-Meadow, Carrie, "Ethics of Compromise," in *Global Encyclopedia of Public Administration, Public Policy and Governance*, A. Farazmand, ed. (Cham: Springer International Publishing 2016).

Mnookin, Robert H. and Louis Kornhauser, "Bargaining in the Shadow of the Law: The Case of Divorce," *Yale Law Journal* 88: 950 (1979).

Nalebuff, Barry and Avinash Dixit, *Thinking Strategically* (New York: Norton 1991).

Nash, John F., "The Bargaining Problem," *Econometrica* 18: 155–62 (1950).

Valley, K. L., M. A. Neale, and E. A. Mannix, "Friends, Lovers, Colleagues, Strangers: The Effects of Relationships on the Process and Outcome of Dyadic Negotiations," in *Research on Negotiation in Organizations* 65–93, R. J. Bies, R. J. Lewicki, and B. H. Shepard, eds (Greenwich, CT: JAI Press 1995).

Chapter 3: Contexts in negotiation

Alkon, Cynthia and Andrea Kupfer Schneider, *Negotiating Crime: Plea Bargaining, Problem Solving and Dispute Resolution in the Criminal Context* (Durham, NC: Carolina Press 2019).

Ayres, Ian, "Further Evidence of Discrimination in New Car Negotiations and Estimates of its Cause," *Michigan Law Review* 94: 109 (1995).

Babcock, Linda and Sara Laschever, *Women Don't Ask: Negotiation and the Gender Divide* (Princeton: Princeton University Press 2003).

Brett, Jeanne M., *Negotiating Globally: How to Negotiate Deals, Resolve Disputes and Make Decisions Across Cultural Boundaries* (San Francisco: Jossey Bass 2001).

Elster, Jon, "Strategic Uses of Argument," in *Barriers to Conflict Resolution*, K. Arrow, R. H. Mnookin, L. Ross, A. Tversky, and R. Wilson, eds (New York: W. W. Norton 1995).

Gifford, Donald G., "A Context-Based Theory of Strategy Selection in Legal Negotiation," *Ohio State Law Journal* 46: 41 (1985).

Green, Michael Z., "Negotiating While Black," in *The Negotiator's Desk Reference*, Chris Honeyman and Andrea Kupfer Schneider, eds (St Paul, MN: DRI Press 2017).

Huang, Jeannie and Corinne Low, "Trumping Norms: Lab Evidence on Aggressive Communications before and after 2016 US Presidential Election," *American Economic Review* (January 2017).

Kolb, Deborah, *The Shadow Negotiation: How Women Can Master the Hidden Agenda in Bargaining* (San Francisco: Jossey-Bass Wiley 2000).

Lederach, John Paul, "Cultivating Peace: A Practitioner's View of Deadly Conflict and Negotiation," in *Contemporary Peacemaking: Conflict, Violence and Peace Processes*, J. Darby and R. MacGinty, eds (New York: Palgrave Macmillan 2003).

Meerts, Paul, *Diplomatic Negotiation: Essence and Evolution* (The Hague: Clingendael Institute 2019).

Meltsner, Michael and Philip G. Schrag, "Negotiation," in *Public Interest Advocacy* (Boston: Little Brown 1974).

Menkel-Meadow, Carrie, "Legal Negotiation: A Study of Strategies in Search of a Theory," *American Bar Foundation Research Journal* (1983): 905.

Noesner, Gary, *Stalling for Time: My Life as an FBI Negotiator* (New York: Random House 2018).

Stone, Douglas, Bruce Patton, and Sheila Heen, *Difficult Conversations: How to Discuss What Matters Most* (New York: Penguin 2000).

Thomas, Kenneth, "Conflict and Conflict Management," in *Handbook of Industrial and Organizational Psychology*, Marvin D. Dunnette, ed. (Chicago: Rand McNally College Publishing Company 1976).

Vivet, Emmanuel, ed., *Landmark Negotiations from Around the World: Lessons for Modern Diplomacy* (Cambridge: Intersentia 2019).

Zartman, William, "The Timing of Peace Initiatives: Hurting Stalemates and Ripe Moments," in *Contemporary Peacemaking: Conflict, Violence and Peace Processes*, J. Darby and R. MacGinty, eds (New York: Palgrave Macmillan 2003).

Chapter 4: Behavioral choices in negotiation: What to do and why

Berkel, Georg, *Learning to Negotiate* (Cambridge: Cambridge University Press 2021).

Galinsky, A. D. and T. Mussweiler, "First Offers as Anchors: The Role of Perspective Taking and Negotiator Focus," *Journal of Personality & Social Psychology* 81 (4): 657–69 (2001).

Kolb, Deborah, "Staying in the Game or Changing it: An Analysis of *Moves* and *Turns* in Negotiation," *Negotiation Journal* doi:10.1111/j.0748-4526.2004.00000.x. April 2004: 253–68.

Malhotra, Deepak and Max Bazerman, *Negotiation Genius: How to Overcome Obstacles and Achieve Brilliant Results at the Bargaining Table and Beyond* (New York: Bantam Press 2007).

Menkel-Meadow, Carrie, "Know When to Show Your Hand," *Negotiation Newsletter* 10 (6): 1–4 (Cambridge, MA: Program on Negotiation Harvard University Law School 2007).

Menkel-Meadow, Carrie and Robert Dingwall, "Scripts: What to do When Big Bad Companies Won't Negotiate," in *The Negotiator's Desk Reference*, Christopher Honeyman and Andrea Kupfer Schneider, eds (Washington DC: ABA Press 2017).

Osborne, Alex Faickney, *Applied Imagination: Principles and Procedures of Creative Problem Solving* (New York: Charles Scribner's Sons, 3rd edn 1963).

Pruitt, Dean, Jeffrey Rubin, and Sung Hee Kim, *Social Conflict, Escalation, Stalemate and Settlement* (New York: McGraw-Hill, 3rd edn 2003).

Public International Law and Policy Group, *The International Negotiations Handbook: Success Through Preparation, Strategy and Planning* (Washington DC: Baker & McKenzie 2007).

Susskind, Lawrence, *Good for You, Great for Me: Finding the Trading Zone and Winning at Win–Win Negotiation* (New York: Public Affairs 2014).

Ury, William, *Getting Past No: Negotiating in Difficult Situations* (New York: Bantam Books 1991).

Wheeler, Michael, *The Art of Negotiation: How to Improvise Agreement in a Chaotic World* (New York: Simon & Schuster 2013).

Cialdini, Robert B., *Influence: The Psychology of Persuasion* (New York: William Morrow, rev. edn 1993).

Freshman, Clark, Adele Hayes, and Greg Feldman, "The Negotiator as Mood Scientist: What We Know and Don't Know About How Mood Relates to Successful Negotiation," *J. Dispute Resolution* (2002).

Gardner, Howard, *Frames of Mind: The Theory of Multiple Intelligences* (London: Hachette 2011).

Gilovich, Thomas and Lee Ross, *The Wisest One in the Room: How You Can Benefit from Social Psychology's Most Powerful Insights* (New York: Free Press 2015).

Greenwald, Anthony and Linda Hamilton Krieger, "Implicit Bias: Scientific Foundations," *California Law Review* 94: 945–67 (2006).

Implicit Bias Test: <https://implicit.harvard.edu/implicit/takeatest.html>.

Kahneman, Daniel, *Thinking Fast and Thinking Slow* (New York: Farrar, Straus and Giroux 2011).

Kahneman, Daniel, Olivier Sibony, and Cass Sunstein, *Noise: A Flaw in Human Judgment* (New York: Little Brown & Co. 2021).

Kiser, Randall, *How Leading Lawyers Think: Expert Insights into Judgment and Advocacy* (Berlin: Springer 2011).

Lewis, Michael, *Moneyball: The Art of Winning an Unfair Game* (New York: W. W. Norton 2003).

Plott, Charles and Kathryn Zeiler, "Exchange Asymmetries Incorrectly Interpreted as Evidence of Endowment Effect Theory and Prospect Theory," *American Economic Review* 97: 1449–66 (2007).

Raiffa, Howard, with John Richardson and David Metcalf, *Negotiation Analysis: The Science and Art of Collaborative Decision Making* (Cambridge, MA: Harvard University Press 2002).

Robbennolt, Jennifer and Jean Sternlight, *Psychology for Lawyers* (Washington DC: ABA Press, 2nd edn. 2021).

Ross, Lee and Richard Nisbett, *The Person and the Situation: Perspectives of Social Psychology* (London: Pinter & Martin Ltd 2011).

Schelling, Thomas, *The Strategy of Conflict* (Cambridge, MA: Harvard University Press 1960).

Steele, Claude, S. J. Spencer, and Joshua Aronson, "Contending with Group Image: The Psychology of Stereotype and Social Identity Threat," in *Advances in Experimental Social Psychology* 34: 379–440, Mark Zanna, ed. (New York: Academic Press 2002).

Taylor, Shelley E., *Positive Illusions: Creative Self-Deception and the Healthy Mind* (New York: Basic Books 1989).

Chapter 6: Complex multi-party multi-issue negotiations

Elster, Jon, "Strategic Uses of Argument," in *Barriers to Conflict Resolution*, K. Arrow, A. Tversky, L. Ross, R. H. Mnookin, and R. Wilson, eds (New York: W. W. Norton 1995).

Hofstede, Geert, Gert Van Hofstede, and Michael Minkov, *Cultures and Organizations: Software of the Mind* (London: McGraw Hill, 3rd edn 2010).

Janis, Irving L., *Groupthink: Psychological Studies of Policy Decisions and Fiascos* (Boston: Houghton Mifflin, 2nd edn 1982).

Menkel-Meadow, Carrie, "Conflict Resolution by the Numbers," *Negotiation Journal* 31: 317–22 (2017).

Menkel-Meadow, Carrie, ed., *Multi-Party Dispute Resolution, Democracy and Decision Making* (Farnham: Ashgate 2012).

Menkel-Meadow, Carrie, "Negotiating the American Constitution (1787–89): Coalitions, Process Rules and Compromises," in *Landmark Negotiations from Around the World: Lessons for Modern Diplomacy*, E. Vivet, ed. (Cambridge: Intersentia 2019).

Mnookin, Robert H., "Strategic Barriers to Dispute Resolution: A Comparison of Bi-lateral and Multi-Lateral Negotiations," *J. of Institutional and Theoretical Economics* 159: 199–220 (2003).

Raiffa, Howard, "Voting," in *Negotiation Analysis: The Science and Art of Collaborative Decision Making*, H. Raiffa with J. Richardson and D. Metcalf, eds (Cambridge, MA: Belknap Press of Harvard University Press 2002).

Sebenius, James K., "Sequencing to Build Coalitions: With Whom Should I Talk First? In *Wise Choices, Decisions, Games and Negotiations*, Richard Zeckhauser, Ralph L. Keeney, and James K. Sebenius, eds (Boston: Harvard Business School Press 1996).

Siracusa, Joseph M., *Diplomacy: A Very Short Introduction* (Oxford: Oxford University Press 2010).

Stanton, Frederick, *Great Negotiations: Agreements that Changed the Modern World* (Yardley, PA: Westholme Press 2010).

Sunstein, Cass R., "Deliberative Troubles: Why Groups Go to Extremes," *Yale Law Journal* 110: 71–106 (2000).

Susskind, Lawrence, Sarah McKearnan, and Jennifer Thomas-Larmer, *The Consensus Building Handbook: A Comprehensive Guide to Reaching Agreement* (Thousand Oaks, CA: Sage Publications 1999).

Susskind, Lawrence and Jeffrey Cruikshank, *Breaking Robert's Rules: The New Way to Run your Meeting, Build Consensus and Get Results* (New York: Oxford University Press 2006).

Thompson, Leigh, "Multi-Party Negotiations," in *The Mind and the Heart of the Negotiator* (Saddle River, NJ: Prentice Hall, 5th edn 2012).

Chapter 7: Ethical and legal issues in negotiation: Making enforceable agreements

Applbaum, Arthur Isak, *Ethics for Adversaries* (Princeton: Princeton University Press 1999).

Ariely, Dan, *The Honest Truth about Dishonesty: How We Lie to Everyone, Especially Ourselves* (New York: Harper Perennial 2013).

Bazerman, Max and Ann E. Tenbrunsel, *Blind Spots: Why We Fail to Do What's Right and What to Do About It* (Princeton: Princeton University Press 2013).

Bok, Sissela, *Lying: Moral Choice in Public and Private Life* (New York: Vintage, 2nd edn. 1999).

Carr, Alfred Z., "Is Business Bluffing Ethical?" *Harvard Business Review* 46: 143 (1968).

Cohen, Jonathan, "When People are the Means: Negotiating With Respect," *Georgetown Journal of Legal Ethics* 14: 739 (2001).

Gutmann, Amy and Dennis Thompson, *The Spirit of Compromise: Why Governing Demands It and Campaigning Undermines It* (Princeton: Princeton University Press 2014).

Korobkin, Russell, "The Role of Law in Settlement," in *Handbook of Dispute Resolution*, M. Moffitt and R. Bordone, eds (San Francisco: Jossey Bass 2005).

Korobkin, Russell, "Behavioral Ethics, Deception and Legal Negotiation," *Nevada Law Journal* 20: 1209 (2020).

Lewicki, Roy L. and Robert J. Robinson, "Ethical and Unethical Bargaining Tactics: An Empirical Study," *Journal of Business Ethics* 17: 665–82 (1998).

Menkel-Meadow, Carrie and Michael Wheeler, eds, *What's Fair? Ethics for Negotiators* (San Francisco: Jossey-Bass Wiley 2004).

Menkel-Meadow, Carrie, "The Morality of Compromise," in
Negotiator's Desk Reference, Christopher Honeyman and Andrea
Kupfer Schneider, eds (St Paul, MN: DRI Press 2017).

Mnookin, Robert H., *Bargaining with the Devil: When to Negotiate,
When to Fight* (New York: Simon & Schuster 2010).

Pennock, Roland and John Chapman, *NOMOS: Compromise in
Ethics, Law and Politics* (New York: NYU Press 1979).

Shell, Richard G., *Bargaining for Advantage: Negotiation Strategies
for Reasonable People* (New York: Viking, 2nd edn 2006).

Shell, Richard G., *Code of Conscience: Lead with your Values, Advance
your Career* (New York: Harper Collins 2021).

Wetlaufer, Gerald B., "The Ethics of Lying in Negotiation," *Iowa Law
Review* 75: 1219–26 (1990).

White, James J., "Machiavelli and the Bar: Ethical Limitations on
Lying in Negotiation," *American Bar Foundation Research Journal*
(1980): 926.

Chapter 8: The future of negotiation

Amsler, Lisa Blomgren, Janet Martinez, and Stephanie Smith, *Dispute
System Design: Preventing, Managing and Resolving Conflict*
(Palo Alto, CA: Stanford University Press 2020).

Bell, Christine, *On the Law of Peace: Peace Agreements and the Lex
Pacificatoria* (Oxford: Oxford University Press 2008).

Council on Foreign Relations, *Global Conflict Tracker* <https://www.
cfr.org/global-conflict-trackers/?category=us>.

Creutzfeldt, Naomi, *Ombudsmen and ADR: A Comparative Study of
Informal Justice in Europe* (London: Palgrave 2018).

Curran, Daniel, James K. Sebenius, and Michael Watkins, "Two Paths
to Peace: Contrasting George Mitchell in Northern Ireland with
Richard Holbrooke in Bosnia-Herzegovina," *Negotiation Journal*
20: 513–31 (2004).

European Union Regulation 524/2013 Online Dispute Resolution for
Consumer Disputes. May 21, 2013.

Hampshire, Stuart, *Justice is Conflict* (Princeton: Princeton University
Press 2000).

Harter, Philip J., "Negotiating Regulations: A Cure for the Malaise,"
Georgetown Law Journal 71: 1 (1982).

Katsh, Ethan and Orna Rabinovich-Einy, *Digital Justice: Technology
and the Internet of Disputes* (Oxford: Oxford University Press 2017).

Kremenyuk, Victor, *International Negotiation: Analysis, Approaches Issues* (San Francisco: Jossey-Bass 2002).

Menkel-Meadow, Carrie, "Legal Negotiation in Popular Culture: What Are We Bargaining For?," in *Law and Popular Culture*, Michael Freeman, ed. (Oxford: Oxford University Press 2004).

Menkel-Meadow, Carrie, "Why Hasn't the World Gotten to Yes? An Appreciation and Some Reflections," *Negotiation Journal* 22 (3): 485–503 (2006).

Menkel-Meadow, Carrie, "The Historical Contingencies of Conflict Resolution," *International Journal of Conflict Engagement and Resolution* 1: 32–54 (2013).

Moscati, Maria Federica, Michael Palmer, and Marion Roberts, eds, *Comparative Dispute Resolution* (Cheltenham: Edward Elgar 2020).

Putnam, Robert D., "Diplomacy and Domestic Politics: The Logic of Two-Level Games," in *Double-Edge Diplomacy: International Bargaining and Domestic Politics*, R. D. Putnam, P. B. Evans, and H. K. Jacobson, eds (Berkeley: University of California Press, 1993).

Richmond, Oliver P., *Peace: A Very Short Introduction* (Oxford: Oxford University Press 2014).

Schmitz, Amy and Colin Rule, *The New Handshake: Online Dispute Resolution and the Future of Consumer Protection* (Washington DC: American Bar Association Press 2018).

Index

For the benefit of digital users, indexed terms that span two pages (e.g., 52–53) may, on occasion, appear on only one of those pages.

Negotiation

INTERNATIONAL RELATIONS
A Very Short Introduction
Paul Wilkinson

Of undoubtable relevance today, in a post-9-11 world of growing political tension and unease, this *Very Short Introduction* covers the topics essential to an understanding of modern international relations. Paul Wilkinson explains the theories and the practice that underlies the subject, and investigates issues ranging from foreign policy, arms control, and terrorism, to the environment and world poverty. He examines the role of organizations such as the United Nations and the European Union, as well as the influence of ethnic and religious movements and terrorist groups which also play a role in shaping the way states and governments interact. This up-to-date book is required reading for those seeking a new perspective to help untangle and decipher international events.

DIPLOMACY
A Very Short Introduction
Joseph M. Siracusa

Like making war, diplomacy has been around a very long time, at least since the Bronze Age. It was primitive by today's standards, there were few rules, but it was a recognizable form of diplomacy. Since then, diplomacy has evolved greatly, coming to mean different things, to different persons, at different times, ranging from the elegant to the inelegant. Whatever one's definition, few could doubt that the course and consequences of the major events of modern international diplomacy have shaped and changed the global world in which we live. Joseph M. Siracusa introduces the subject of diplomacy from a historical perspective, providing examples from significant historical phases and episodes to illustrate the art of diplomacy in action.

'Professor Siracusa provides a lively introduction to diplomacy through the perspective of history.'

Gerry Woodard, Senior Fellow in Political Science at the University of Melbourne and former Australasian Ambassador in Asia

www.oup.com/vsi